From the book

THE LIGHT WAS DIM, so I put my face close
to the plate for a look. I made out small black shapes
and slightly larger white spots. Ants and ant eggs! Not
wanting to insult my hosts, who had gone to great trouble,
I took a good-sized spoonful, closed my eyes, and feigned
delight. It may have helped that I was hungry, but the ants
were rather tasty with a sort of vinegar-and-nut taste. Still,
I could not get it out of my mind that I was eating insects.
Knowing this was new for me, my hosts asked how I liked it.
"*Mumpia!*" I said with enthusiasm. Delicious. Word
spread immediately.

Ants for Breakfast

Archaeological Adventures Among the Kalinga

James Skibo

THE UNIVERSITY OF UTAH PRESS

Salt Lake City

© 1999 by the University of Utah Press
All rights reserved
99 00 01 02 03 04 05 06
5 4 3 2

LIBRARY OF CONGRESS CATALOGING-IN-PUBLICATION DATA

Skibo, James M.
　　Ants for breakfast : archaeological adventures among the Kalinga /
James Skibo.
　　　　p.　　　cm.
　　Includes bibliographical references.
　　ISBN 0-87480-620-8
　　1. Kalinga (Philippine people) 2. Skibo, James M.
3. Ethnoarchaeology—Philippines—Field work. 4. Ethnology—
Philippines—Field work. I. Title.
DS666.K3S53　1999
392.3'09599—dc21　　　　　　　　　　　　　　99-40540

Contents

Preface   vii

1. Living Archaeology   1

2. Funerals Are Fun   32

3. Once Were Headhunters   61

4. Ants for Breakfast   84

5. The Bamboo Classroom   109

6. "Are We in Danger?"   127

7. What Goes in Must Come Out   142

8. Kalinga Justice   156

9. When a Town Gets a Road the People Go Crazy   164

Bibliography   169

Acknowledgments   177

About the Author   179

Preface

I LIVED WITH THE KALINGA to undertake anthropological fieldwork—specifically ethnoarchaeology—but this is not a scientific report. This book is about life with the Kalinga and the lessons I took with me. Although I was in the Philippines for just four months, that short time was packed with the elements of a good thriller: mystery, danger, sex, violence, death.

Since 1988, when the project was active, I have come to realize that my time with the Kalinga was a defining moment. Like most anthropologists, I found that living with traditional, non-Western peoples was an opportunity to taste a world both subtly and vastly different, while offering a new perspective on my own.

The Kalinga are wet-rice agriculturalists living in the rugged mountains of northern Luzon. They have much to offer. Although they are headhunters and the blood feud continues to this day, in many ways they are more "civilized" than Western societies. A good example is the way that the Kalinga deal with serious crime. In our society a woman who is raped is often a victim twice: once at the hands of the rapist and again as a participant in our often-harsh judicial system. I witnessed the prosecution of a Kalinga rape case, and within three days of the crime a group of community elders determined a punishment for the rapist and provided the victim with a large cash compensation. In any culture rape is a brutal act of violence, but I was struck by the way it was handled and how well and quickly the victim appeared to recover from the ordeal. All societies struggle to solve problems of crime, disorderly conduct, health care, mental illness, and inequality, to name a few. As Americans enter the twenty-first century with these problems yet unresolved, it might be worthwhile to set aside our notions of cultural superiority and take a peek at how others deal with the same issues.

I felt compelled to write this book for another reason, as well. Most scientific writing today is so specialized that it is inaccessible to the general public. I believe that all scientists and certainly all archaeologists have an obligation to spend some energy making their work accessible. Archaeology will never cure the common cold or build something that benefits the common good. Introductory archaeology textbooks often say that archaeology is important because it is wise to learn and understand our past; our own life experiences teach us that learning from past mistakes helps chart a better and brighter future. Archaeologists have studied the rise and fall of hundreds of past civilizations, but I don't recall ever getting a call from a politician who wanted to know everything about the Classic Maya collapse before signing a treaty or voting against an environmental protection law. Some general findings do trickle down and eventually have an effect on global decision making but only in the most indirect way.

So what justifies archaeology? Simply, people are interested. Archaeology is a unique discipline, unlike chemistry or physics, in that ordinary people as well as specialists are interested in it. There are the ubiquitous cable-TV shows. And every archaeologist can tell of encounters at cocktail parties, on airplanes, or in the dentist's chair when the follow-up to "What do you do?" is "I always wanted to be an archaeologist." The farmer, construction worker, car maker, engineer, mechanic, and homemaker are the ones watching the nightly archaeology shows and pondering what came before. How did humans evolve? Who made the first tool? Who lit the first fire? How did ancient hunters bring down giant Ice Age mammals, and why did people start growing corn, wheat, and rice instead of continuing to hunt and gather as they had for millions of years? Why did civilizations develop and why did they collapse? This is the lure of archaeology.

As a university-employed archaeologist, I have learned that not everything about archaeology is interesting to nonspecialists, but some things do inspire and excite students. These are the stories we should be telling to the public.

Here, I aim to demystify the process of archaeology and ethnographic fieldwork. While there are some truths in the Indiana Jones film trilogy, it is a safe assumption that most people have little idea what present-day archaeologists really do. In one of the first scenes of *Raiders of the Lost Ark*, Dr. Jones says that most of the exciting archaeological finds today are made in the library. Many if not most of today's important discoveries do indeed occur as the result of tedious laboratory or library research, but all archaeologists can speak to the thrill of discovery, of unearthing a house used five thousand years ago, and like Indiana Jones some have even clambered over rope bridges and dodged bullets.

A final reason for this story is because of the encouragement of my wife, Becky. She joined me for part of the project and by the time we returned to Tucson was already saying I should write about it. She finally convinced me in the fall of 1994, six years later. Indeed, it is from our journals and letters that I am able to recall the details of many events. Her unique perspective on many of the same events enriches this story.

CHAPTER 1

Living Archaeology

We WALKED CAUTIOUSLY into the Manila Hilton on a sticky
June afternoon. After months of fieldwork in the mountains of the
Philippines, sleeping on bamboo floors, eating with our hands, and
living without indoor plumbing, my wife and I felt we deserved
some luxury. Our sandals, tattered clothes, and weathered backpacks were conspicuous as we crossed the plush carpeting beneath
glass chandeliers. The Manila Hilton, one of the city's finest hotels,
had seen many distinguished guests, including Muhammad Ali and
his entourage during the Thrilla in Manila, his legendary heavy-
weight title match with Joe Frazier. The armed guards and the
woman behind the desk eyed us suspiciously, but I triumphantly
pulled out my American Express card and got us a room for our
last two nights in the Philippines.

We justified this short stay at the Hilton as a means to ease our
transition back into life in the United States. When bathing entails
dumping buckets of cold water on one's body, the average washing
time might be two minutes; this day we let the hot water run over
our bodies until our skin puckered. After the steam cleared, I saw
myself in the full-length mirror.

I looked like hell. My hair stuck out in unnatural ways—the
result of cutting it myself with the aid of a metal signal mirror—and
my pale, gaunt body was startling. The image was more like Abe
Lincoln after Gettysburg than the person who had started this project
over four months earlier. More than a month of dysentery had taken
its toll. The only thing keeping me going was a concoction of almost
pure electrolytes that tasted like melted aluminum. Still, emaciation

notwithstanding, I felt a sense of real accomplishment. We had collected enough data to complete my dissertation, had survived the outbreak of tribal war and run-ins with communist insurgents, and had gotten to know a people who changed our lives forever.

My involvement in the Philippine project had begun over a year earlier and thousands of miles away on the campus of the University of Arizona in Tucson. The beginning of the fall semester in the anthropology graduate program at the University of Arizona is always an exciting time. Faculty members and students return from the Near East, China, South America, and other far-away lands with tales of adventure and discovery. The hallways and coffee shops buzz with stories about kiva excavations in northern Arizona, near misses with rattlesnakes, searching for Inca sites in the mountains of Peru, and fighting bouts with amebic dysentery. (Anthropological fieldwork can be a permanent cure for constipation.)

In the fall of 1986 Professor Bill Longacre was returning from a summer's fieldwork in the Philippines. Longacre, a preeminent authority on archaeological pottery, had devoted the early part of his career to excavating pueblos in the American Southwest before turning his attention to the Philippines. He had spent a year living and working with the Kalinga people during 1975 and 1976, but for the first time in several years he was able to visit the Kalinga again. Earlier in 1986, Cory Aquino was elected president after the people of the Philippines removed Ferdinand Marcos. In a fashion that is all too common, Marcos and his wife Imelda had used their power to enrich themselves, kin, and associates at their country's expense. Imelda's famous shoe closet, soon on display in the former palace, was a fitting symbol. While many Filipinos outside the palace walls walked barefoot, Imelda possessed hundreds of pairs of shoes purchased from stores around the world.

Located in the Cordillera Mountains, one of the most rugged and isolated areas in the Philippines, the Kalinga were little affected by political decisions emanating from Malacañang Palace. But in 1974 they and the people of the Mountain Province took center stage. Marcos and the National Power Corporation sought to build a series of four dams along a hundred-kilometer stretch of the Chico River for generating hydroelectric power. This decision was made without regard for the thousands of Kalinga and other peoples of the region who stood to lose their homes and land. It was estimated that five thousand Kalinga would be uprooted and thousands of rice fields and fruit trees inundated. The Kalinga, widely known for their aggressiveness, began obstructing some of the early survey efforts. This got the attention of the government, and Kalinga *pangats*, the respected elders, were invited to Malacañang Palace for a meeting with Marcos.

Although the government's offer of land and cash for resettled villagers seemed generous, the Kalinga remained distrustful. The *pangats* traveled to other recently dammed river valleys and found the resettled people living in poverty. In typical Kalinga fashion, the returning *pangats* formed a *bodong*, or peace pact, with the neighboring Bontoc to oppose the dam. The government then attempted to bribe the Kalinga opposition leader Macli-ing with money, a good job, and women to stop the protest. He refused and was shot in his home by government troops.

Macli-ing's murder crystallized Kalinga opposition. In the latter part of 1976 the Kalinga linked their struggle with the New Peoples Army (NPA), a communist group that had gained great momentum during the Marcos era. The military eventually entered the region in force, but the guerrilla tactics of Kalinga warriors, now armed with modern weapons, were very effective in sabotaging any effort at construction. As of 1986 the dams had not been built. Cory Aquino's first act as president was to cancel the Chico River Hydroelectric Project, which brought peace to the area for the first time in a decade.

So there was added excitement as we assembled in a lecture room to hear Bill Longacre's talk. Not only was it safe again to travel into the Kalinga region, but Longacre had been in Manila immediately following the dramatic People Power Revolution. Longacre made his presentation, complete with slide show from his latest trip to Kalingaland. The Kalinga homeland, with its lush vegetation and terraced mountains, was a beguiling contrast to southern Arizona's Sonora Desert. I was spellbound as he discussed his plan for a new, year-long study among the Kalinga. In retrospect, this lecture was an hour-long infomercial for graduate students, but I was hooked. If he had displayed an 800 number I would have been the first on the line, credit card in hand.

Although Longacre was a full professor of anthropology and more than twenty years my senior, we had one thing in common— a passion for pottery. Pottery, or ceramics, is a unique data set. It is made frequently, broken often, and comes in endless varieties according to economic and social requirements. Its appearance worldwide coincides approximately with the beginnings of agriculture and domesticated plants such as corn in the Americas, wheat and barley in the Near East and Europe, and rice in Asia. Cooking pots are essential for effectively processing these foods, in some cases for making them palatable at all.

For the archaeologist, the wonderful thing about pottery is that it not only breaks a lot but it was made by prehistoric people to perform numerous functions. In archaeological sites that postdate the advent of agriculture, pottery sherds, or broken pieces of pottery, are the most commonly found artifact. Consequently, archaeologists have used pottery for virtually every type of inference about the past. Pottery is distributed widely and has a relatively short duration of use; thus it can be used to mark the passage of time, track changes in diet, determine trade routes, and illuminate the status of individuals or communities.

Longacre's involvement in ceramics went back to the 1960s and his highly influential case study for the New Archaeology. New Archaeology, promoted primarily by Lewis Binford in prophet-like fashion, was dedicated to transforming archaeology from a rather antiquarian effort that focused on fact collection and the proper sequencing of prehistoric material into a discipline using archaeological techniques to investigate topics more in the domain of cultural anthropology.

Archaeology in the United States is unique because of its close association with anthropology. In Europe, Japan, and most everywhere else in the world, academic archaeologists work in departments of history or geology. At the beginning of the twentieth century, American anthropologists were busy recording Native American cultures, frequently because they supposed Native Americans were going the way of the buffalo. At many Indian villages researchers found ancient ruins, which they proposed to use as a means to trace the origin and evolution of a particular tribe. To accomplish this goal, they used archaeological techniques of excavation and analysis developed by European prehistorians.

Thus archaeology in the United States became a way to investigate ancient Native Americans. Along with physical anthropology, cultural anthropology, and linguistics, it is one of the four subdisciplines of anthropology. Although one might call it a historical accident that archaeology at American universities is part of anthropology programs, by the 1960s Binford, Longacre, and others intensified the link as they attempted to demonstrate that prehistoric artifacts could be used to infer kinship, social organization, religion, and other topics confined to cultural anthropology and the study of living people.

Longacre was one of the first to put the New Archaeology to work. Beginning with the distribution of pottery types from Carter Ranch, a prehistoric pueblo in Arizona, Longacre attempted to determine whether the group was organized along the mother's or father's family line, as well as the pueblo's postmarital residence patterns—where people live after they marry. Longacre inferred that the prehistoric inhabitants of this pueblo were matrilocal, meaning the husband moved into his wife's village and household after marriage.

Although his work changed archaeological ceramic studies forever, it was fraught with unanswered questions. If archaeologists are to use prehistoric pot sherds to answer anthropological questions, there was a need to learn more about how people make, use, and distribute their pottery. This led Longacre to search for a place where pottery was still made and used. He found the Kalinga, a tribal group of rice agriculturists living in the mountains of the Philippine island of Luzon. Thus he was also one of the first researchers to embark on a new area of study—*ethnoarchaeology*.

An ethnoarchaeologist studies living people to help answer questions archaeologists ask about prehistory. Here one might ask, "Why not use the data collected by cultural anthropologists, like Margaret Mead?" The answer is, they do, but Margaret Mead did not collect the kinds of information useful to archaeologists. Cultural

Carter Ranch Pueblo showing the excavated rooms and a kiva in the northern portion of the site. (Photo courtesy of the Field Museum, Neg. #98414)

anthropologists do not focus on the artifacts, or material culture, of the people. Archaeologists are left with the task of reconstructing past life from the artifacts that remain. Kinship, social organization, economies, and status of individuals do not preserve well, but artifacts do. Ethnoarchaeologists examine the relationships in existing groups between artifacts (like pots, houses, and tools) and things such as diet, demography, and social organization.

One of Lewis Binford's famous studies considered the Nunamiut Eskimo, caribou hunters from northern Alaska, to help archaeologists understand the connections between hunting and butchering practices and the artifacts and bones that are left behind. Archaeologists who study hunter-gatherers, the primary human adaptation for most of our four million years on this planet, must reconstruct prehistoric behavior primarily from patterns observed in the distribution of stone tools and animal bone.

Binford was inspired to perform ethnoarchaeology while studying Neanderthal sites from southern France and the famous Mousterian-period tools dating 40,000 to 100,000 years ago. Some had argued that sites with different types of Mousterian tools and different animal bones reflected various Neanderthal culture groups. (Neanderthals were an archaic form of *Homo sapiens* but apparently not direct ancestors.) Binford questioned this reconstruction

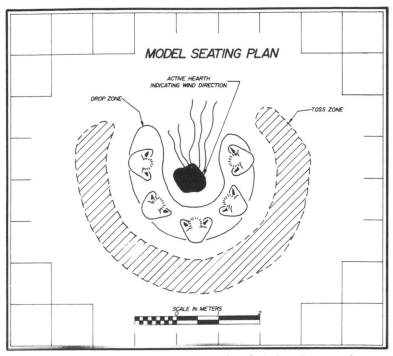

A sketch by Lewis Binford during his ethnoarchaeological work among the Nunamiut Eskimo of Alaska showing how bone is differentially deposited by people sitting around a hearth. The drop zone consists of small bone fragments while the forward and backward areas have larger bones. (Reproduced by permission of Lewis Binford and the Society for American Archaeology from *American Antiquity* 43(3) 1978)

and suggested instead that the variability in stone tools and animal bones at Neanderthal sites could be explained by functional rather than cultural factors. That is, the sites were specialized camps where Neanderthal hunters killed and butchered different types of animals with tool kits designed specifically for that purpose.

Binford was frustrated by the lack of information about the relationship between animal bones found at sites and the behaviors that led to their deposition. So in the early 1970s, he initiated an ethnoarchaeological project among the Nunamiut that focused on animal hunting and processing sites and their associated bone deposits. Obviously modern, Eskimo hunters are not exactly like Neanderthal hunters of 100,000 years ago; the idea, once again, was

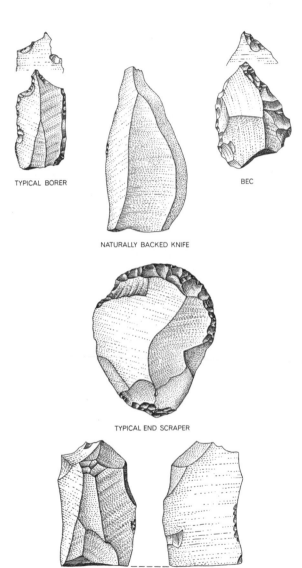

TYPICAL BORER

BEC

NATURALLY BACKED KNIFE

TYPICAL END SCRAPER

ATYPICAL BURIN

Five classes of Mousterian tools made by Neanderthals. According to the analysis by Sally and Lewis Binford, the tools were probably used to make other tools out of bone or wood. (Reproduced by permission of Eric Mose) to seek and understand any general processes governing the connections between people and artifacts.

The Nunamiut ethnoarchaeological research has had a great impact on archaeologists who study hunter-gatherers. Now armed with their own new tools for understanding the causal relations between animal bone remains and human activities, archaeologists can more easily infer the types of behaviors occurring at their excavated sites.

Among the first ethnoarchaeologists to study agricultural and sedentary people was Carol Kramer, who was trained as a Middle Eastern archaeologist. Following the work of Patty Jo Watson, Kramer spent her field seasons excavating sites in what is now Iran and Iraq, where domesticated plants and animals first appeared. During her field seasons she often wandered into the nearby villages, which were quite similar in terms of design and construction materials to the prehistoric sites she was digging. In fact, the local crew members hired by the archaeologists often were quite helpful in puzzling out various features encountered during excavation. Kramer realized that prehistorians could benefit from an extensive ethnoarchaeological study of one of these contemporary Iranian villages.

In 1975, Kramer performed a study of a small Iranian village looking specifically at the types of questions the prehistorians working nearby were asking. For example, she considered household status and material culture, and how population and wealth are reflected in architectural variables such as house size. By living with the people she was able to establish clear links between human behavior and material culture.

This is also what Longacre was attempting during his first trip to the Kalinga village of Dangtalan in 1973.

Besides our affinity for archaeological pottery, Longacre and I had another connection—we were both "Yoopers." Yoopers come from the Upper Peninsula of Michigan, locally referred to as the U.P. Sparsely populated and heavily forested, the Upper Peninsula is home for the descendants of Cornish tin miners, Swedes, Poles, Italians, and Finns who settled there to work the copper and iron mines. What has evolved is a culture with unique food (like the

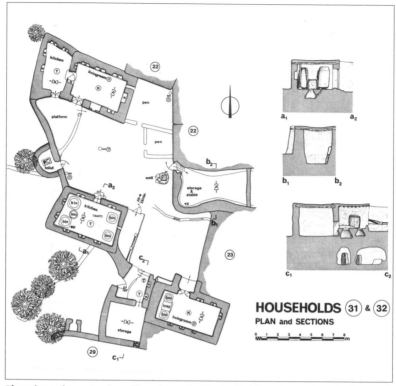

Plan view of two Iranian village households studied by ethnoarchaeologist Carol Kramer. (From *Village Ethnoarchaeology;* reproduced by permission of Academic Press and Carol Kramer)

pastie, a meat, potato, and onion pie), dialect ("garage" is pronounced "crotch"), and lifestyle that revolves around hunting, fishing, and skiing.

Interestingly (to us at least), there also is a high percentage of Yooper archaeologists, though this is probably a function of the low population. Besides Longacre and me, there is Alfred Vincent Kidder, born in 1885 in the important city of Marquette—the Yooper Mecca. Kidder, considered the father of Southwestern archaeology, is best known for his excavation at Pecos Pueblo, New Mexico during the first half of the twentieth century. Using the new concept of stratigraphy, Kidder worked out the cultural sequence of the northern American Southwest. Kidder was instrumental in redefining archaeology in the twentieth century by setting new standards for research that began to bring the discipline out of its traditional antiquarianism. But what is best about our Yooper brother is that he too was a pottery man. His 1914 Harvard dissertation was on Southwestern ceramics.

Although Longacre and I shared a passion for pottery and Yooper pasties, I was still apprehensive as I entered his office during his scheduled office hours. I had taken two of his courses and we shared a Yooper yarn occasionally, but I still called him Dr. Longacre. Twenty years earlier at Arizona's archaeological field school, directed by Longacre, students started calling him "Uncle Willie." All his students since have used the term. At the time, Longacre was a twenty-six-year-old professor, and many of his students (some of them older than he) found it difficult to call him "Doctor." It seemed improper and too informal to call him "Bill," so the compromise "Uncle Willie" soon took hold. It was only a day or so after his lecture, but I was already convinced that I too wanted to be among those who called him "Uncle Willie" and be a part of the Kalinga Ethnoarchaeology Project. I had only to convince him to take me.

Longacre interacted with students in a way that has always been rare among professors—he listened. Most students know that if you ask a professor a question or two he or she can carry on into the wee hours, demanding little from the listener. Longacre's style could be uncomfortable for students more accustomed to the pearls-of-wisdom approach, but I found it good training and have since tried to emulate it with my own students. Still, on that fall afternoon in Tucson, I came armed with a speech. After telling him how much I liked his talk and his proposed study among the Kalinga, I paused, hoping for an invitation. None came. He simply nodded his head, so I launched into a discussion of my activities. For the previous six months I had been working in Michael Schiffer's laboratory on ceramic abrasion and use-wear. Specifically, I was trying to determine how prehistoric pots were used by investigating the scrapes, nicks, and chips that remained on the vessels. I emphasized this area of my research because Longacre had mentioned pottery use-wear as one of the proposed study areas for the upcoming Kalinga project. I pointed out this miraculous convergence and how I hoped to continue my line of research. After a full ten-minute monologue, I paused, and Longacre simply said, "I was hoping you would come in."

Deciding to do a project and getting eager graduate students involved is the easy part; finding funding can be much more difficult, and this is the rock on which many great ideas founder. It would be an expensive project. Funds were needed for airfare to the Philippines for Longacre and five graduate students, living expenses for one year, full-time salary for up to ten Kalinga assistants, travel costs within the Philippines, and money to pay for the collection, transport, and curation of hundreds of pots and baskets, and other items.

Archaeologists receive funding from such organizations as the Wenner-Gren Foundation, the National Geographic Society, and a variety of local government and private foundations. But a project of this size would require funding from the National Science Foundation. Established in the 1950s, the N.S.F. is the major source for basic research in all sciences, including archaeology. Archaeology receives just a minuscule portion of its total funds, but many major archaeological projects by Americans have been funded by the N.S.F. The problem is that in a good year only about 20 percent of the proposals are funded. Each year worthy projects do not make the cut, and many excellent studies never make it beyond the proposal stage.

The key to a successful N.S.F. proposal is having an interesting problem and demonstrating to the reviewers' satisfaction that the project can actually be carried out. Luckily, Longacre could easily cover these two points in the proposal. His previous work among the Kalinga demonstrated how the project would be accomplished, and we were certainly proposing to answer interesting and relevant questions.

Since Longacre's first work in ethnoarchaeology in the 1970s, archaeology had begun to view artifacts as the means to a much finer level of information about the past, rather than simply as items to be curated. Accordingly, the Kalinga project focused on six separate topics: pottery use-life, economics, pottery production and distribution, formation processes, basketry, and pottery use-alteration.

There is an economic foundation to any society, regardless of its complexity. Archaeologists spend a great deal of time trying to reconstruct prehistoric economies from artifacts, and ethnoarchaeology seemed to promise more insight into the various connections between material items and economic system. For example, one of the simple but important questions posed by the Kalinga project was, What is valuable to the Kalinga? Prehistorians can assign value to objects recovered from the past to reconstruct economic systems, but are their assumptions about value accurate? An ethnoarchaeologist looks at a Kalinga village and asks, If this village were abandoned, how could I recreate its economy? Which artifacts would differentiate the richest and poorest households?

Because much of the Kalinga project was focused on pottery, the economic study also addressed whether the wealth of a household could be assessed using ceramic data. For example, do richer households have more pots, bigger pots, different kinds of pots? Brian Trostel, a graduate student from Arizona, asked such questions while he performed the economic study in Dangtalan village. Brian was fond of saying he was the only researcher looking at something that the Kalinga themselves thought was important. He said this in jest but he was correct. The Kalinga, like most traditional pottery makers around the world, placed little value on their ceramic technology though they were quite interested in the value of their possessions (like rice fields or houses). Our fixation on pottery was a matter of some amusement for the Kalinga, and it didn't hurt to have Brian's research coincide with their view of what really matters.

The Kalinga make pottery both for their own use and for sale. Wares that are traded or sold can be found surprisingly far from their source. Prehistorians working around the globe also find pots at their excavations that come from tens, even hundreds, of miles away. How and why these pots traveled such long distances to various prehistoric settlements is a matter of great interest. For example, different kinds of prehistoric social systems, like tribes, chiefdoms, or states, had different levels of pottery production and modes of distribution. Understanding craft production and distribution is a key to unlocking prehistoric economic and social systems and can also shed light on the extent of cultural influence at certain times in the past. So Miriam Stark, also an Arizona graduate student, focused her study on the pottery-producing village of Dalupa to understand how Kalinga women made and distributed their vessels.

An archaeologist's fantasy is to excavate a site like Pompeii, the famous city in Italy covered in volcanic ash by Mount Vesuvius in A.D. 79. Still being exposed, the kitchens, living rooms, and plazas in Pompeii, the largest ongoing archaeological excavation in the world, give us a snapshot of life two millennia ago. But sites like Pompeii are rare. A majority of archaeologists dig in village sites purposely abandoned by inhabitants who took with them the most valuable and useful artifacts. Archaeologists must reconstruct what went on by what was discarded or lost by the long-departed people—their trash. In fact, Alfred Kidder, at his famous Pecos Pueblo dig, made most of his important discoveries by excavating a large trash pile, or *midden*. The midden was used as a dump for hundreds of years, and the layers of artifacts (especially the ceramics because their painted designs varied extremely over time) provided a chronological history of technological and societal change at the pueblo.

Because archaeological sites are more like Pecos than Pompeii, it is worth understanding how people break their objects, where they throw them, and how items decompose and disintegrate. This area of study, called formation processes, was formalized in archaeology by Michael Schiffer, mentioned earlier, and became an integral part of the Kalinga project. The study of formation processes was the province of Christopher Turner.

To make inferences from pottery, one must have a good understanding of how the pots were used. Were the vessels used for cooking, serving, or storing, or were they used for trade or ritual purposes? One of the ways in which the Kalinga project explored this question was by investigating things such as food residues and the scratches and chips that could indicate what functions a vessel might have served. If a prehistorian had a method to determine pottery use from traces left in a vessel, then his or her reconstruction of the past would be on firmer ground. While this seems obvious, an insight from ethnoarchaeological research is that pottery often serves purposes far different from those for which it was originally intended. Masashi Kobayashi and I collaborated on the pottery use-alteration project in the village of Guina-ang.

A cross-section of the excavated midden at Pecos Pueblo. (From *An Introduction to Southwestern Prehistory* by A.V. Kidder; reproduced by permission of Yale University Press)

Pottery, it must be allowed, is not the only significant type of material culture, nor was it the sole focus of the Kalinga project. One of the researchers, Ramon Silvestre, an Arizona graduate student but also a Filipino, initiated the first ethnoarchaeological study of Kalinga basketry. In contrast to pottery, which in Kalinga society is made by women, basketry is primarily a male technology. The Kalinga are wonderful basket weavers; they not only make many varieties of baskets but also weave backpacks, pouches, chicken cages, and even the walls for their houses.

Aside from coordinating the project, Longacre also proposed to continue his own research on pottery use-life. As mentioned, Kidder used frequencies of pot sherds found in the Pecos trash midden to document change through time. A modern research refinement, however, is the pot's use-life. Some vessels, such as everyday cooking pots, typically last less than a year while others can last decades. Obviously, the vessels that break often would be disproportionately represented in prehistoric trash. Longacre focused on understanding how long different types of vessels last.

Jose Lorde Villamor (Jojo), then a graduate student at the University of the Philippines, also participated in the project, but he performed a cultural anthropology study that focused on rice-field construction. Kalinga build terraced rice fields on hillsides irrigated by mountain springs. Rice is the Kalinga staple, with fields owned individually, so this too was research the Kalinga people found worthy.

Longacre had to put all these ideas into a neat package and sell them to the N.S.F. He must have done a great job because we received high marks for the proposal from a panel of six peer reviewers. Better, the N.S.F. agreed to provide funds. After a whirlwind of preparatory activity, and I found myself sitting in a jeep traveling to the Kalinga homeland.

The trip north to Kalinga was a journey through time. I started out in the traffic-clogged city of Manila, but traveling through the countryside and small communities I witnessed a transformation. The Philippine countryside was as beautiful as Manila was bleak. Manila was congested, brown with pollution, and fast-paced, whereas the rural north surprised me with its beauty and tranquility. My lungs started to recover from a week of Manila air as we traveled through rice fields and small towns. There were notable changes in the people as well. As we bounced deeper into the mountains, I began to witness the great cultural diversity of the Philippines, a country composed of over seven thousand islands, hundreds of different cultural groups, and many languages. I saw my first carabao, the docile water buffalo used in tilling rice fields, moving slowly through a field. It was February and the rice, planted in individual family plots, was just beginning to mature. The road north was a major highway, but people who lived nearby found its surface perfect for drying rice. Our driver from the National Museum had several near misses with boulders that the locals put in the roadway so that autos would not drive over their grain.

I pictured myself in the mode of Alfred Kidder. Archaeology in early twentieth-century Colorado, Utah, New Mexico, or Arizona was not just finding sites and digging up ruins, it was an adventure in which one experienced frontier life and lived among native peoples. Kidder, coming from Harvard, traveled to western towns like Durango, Cortez, and Bluff, which were probably not all that different from the Filipino towns I was now passing through.

Rice fields and countryside: a welcome contrast to urban Manila. (James Skibo)

The docile carabao. (James Skibo)

In his first journey west Kidder was more impressed by the adventure of the new land than with the archaeology work before him. He traveled by train, wagon, and horse rather than by jeep and on foot, but I felt I shared his fascination with native peoples and an appreciation for the natural wonders that surrounded us. In Durango, Kidder sat on the front porch of the Palace Hotel watching ranchers and Indians pass by. He noted in his later writings that they included an "Apache wrapped in a blanket, his black hair in two braids."

After nine hours we arrived in the province of Cagayan, the homeland of Ferdinand Marcos and possibly the only place in the Philippines where he was popular to the end. Bill, as I now called Dr. Longacre, Masashi, Jojo, assistants, and I spent the night in Tuguegarao at the Hotel Delfino, accommodations nicer than those we had in Manila. I quickly saw the advantage of staying at the same hotel as Bill. Although it was riveted with bullet holes, the result of a recent assassination attempt on the hotel owner, who was also Tuguegarao's mayor, the place had good food, a disco, plus one surprise—a telephone with overseas access.

I thought to surprise Becky with a phone call. She was scheduled to join me in several months and would not expect to hear from me except by letter, which reportedly took two to three weeks. In retrospect, the phone call was a mistake—I ruined both her day and mine. I gave the hotel our home number and they tried unsuccessfully all evening to connect with an overseas operator. The following morning someone came to my room to announce that the hotel had finally gotten through to an overseas operator. The connection was not good and it was like using a C.B. radio because only one person could talk at a time.

I had left Tucson three weeks earlier and had much to tell her, but little could be said. I hung up after the short conversation feeling lonely and depressed. I went to my room and sat well into the night. Since our marriage several years earlier, we had never been separated for any length of time. Some couples do better at this, but we seemed to be struggling. I do not recall reading that Alfred Kidder suffered when separated from loved ones. Did he have a lover back at Cambridge? Staring at the ceiling of my room that night, I questioned whether I was cut out for the life of adventure.

Next morning, preparations for our continued journey pulled me from my funk. The museum's vehicle and driver would return to Manila, leaving us to find our own transportation for the re mainder of the trip. We spent the day buying supplies and arranging transportation to Tabuk, the provincial capital of Kalinga-Apayao. Vehicles, referred to as "jeepnies," made the trip from Tuguegarao to Tabuk on a regular basis, and one could get a seat for a few pesos. But we had so many supplies and people that we required our own jeepney and driver.

Jeepnies are one of the main forms of transportation in the Philippines. When Douglas MacArthur fulfilled his pledge to return to the Philippines near the end of World War II, he found a country in shambles. The Filipino transportation system had been destroyed, so the U.S. military provided jeeps refitted to carry more people. Today the descendants of the original jeeps, garishly decorated, clog Manila streets and are found throughout the country. In the provincial towns, however, the primary form of public transportation is the "tricie"—a small motorcycle with a covered sidecar. Like ants scurrying along a trail, hundreds of tricies weave through the streets with a purpose known only to their drivers.

Jeepnies, seen here in Manila. (James Skibo)

A tricie, in this case filled with pots. (William Longacre)

My first ride in a tricie was with Bill Longacre that morning in Tuguegarao. Though I had seen as many as four Filipinos ride in a sidecar, the driver shook his head in astonishment as Bill and I, each weighing over 200 pounds, tried to fit in the cramped space. After Bill there remained just four inches of seat, but I dove in with enthusiasm, feeling the sides of the tricie bulge. The driver seemed to think this was quite amusing until he noticed that the front wheel of the motorcycle was off the ground, making it impossible to steer. With a leg and an arm hanging out the side and my head wedged against the top canopy, the driver moved up to sit on the gas tank to counterbalance our weight and gunned the tiny engine, which consented after a second or two.

The following day we set out for the short trip to Tabuk, a relatively uneventful several-hour ride through a picturesque valley. Tabuk was everything one would expect in an outpost town. Many Kalinga aspire to live in Tabuk because it has electricity, markets, a medical clinic, and better schools, but it was also a town struggling with modernization and growth. The unpaved streets were muddy during the rainy season, and the choking dust of the dry season was hardly an improvement. Electrical wires, put up helter-skelter by anyone with wire and the will, sagged overhead, bare ends exposed at every junction. Electrified houses, no doubt hooked up without actually turning off the juice, were a status symbol. I wondered about fire, as I looked up at the looped-wire connections.

Most exciting for me were the Kalinga filling the streets; some dressed in business suits and employed by the government, others walking barefoot with large machetes called *bolos* strapped to their sides. The mix of traditional and modern, businessmen and head-hunters, teachers and rice farmers, medical doctors and tribal healers, heightened my sense of having arrived at the edge. For most Kalinga, Tabuk was the only city they would ever visit. It seemed a fascinating case of culture mixing, perhaps a good place for research, but our destination was the Pasil River Valley, a full day's ride into the mountains.

Immediately after leaving Tabuk, jeepney piled high with supplies and people, we started to ascend the Cordillera Mountains, one of the most rugged and remote locations on the island of Luzon.

Our jeepney, in this case a vehicle made by Ford, climbed the hills slowly, following a narrow road carved into the side of the mountain. The ride would have been pleasant had the dust not poured into the open sides of the vehicle every time it slowed for a curve or hill. Within minutes everything and everybody was covered with dust, the dark hair of the Filipino students and assistants now a sandy color. We all covered our noses and mouths with scarves or tied bandannas around our faces, making us look like train robbers in movie westerns.

I found relief by climbing on the roof of the vehicle, when it was moving, and clinging precipitously to the supplies lashed on top. Despite the low branches it was the best seat. The majestic views of the Chico River Valley, Marcos's favored dam and reservoir site, were breathtaking, and the tropical forest was so outrageously green that it almost hurt my eyes.

At a fork in the road, about halfway in our journey, we turned away from the river valley and headed up a road even narrower and steeper. At times one side of the jeepney nearly scraped the wall of the mountainside while the other wheel came within inches of the escarpment. My crow's nest seat gave me a clear view not only of the scenery but also of our harrowing trail, which was in a state of perpetual reconstruction because of frequent mud slides. As we passed particularly dangerous spots, Bill's Kalinga assistants, who had joined us at Tabuk, would "recall" stories of jeepnies plunging over the side during one slide or another. These stories, which grew more frequent as we inched closer to the Pasil River Valley, were interrupted only to inform us *sotto voce* that we were approaching an area that was common for "holduppers."

Resistance to the proposed dam had brought many more guns into the area; some of these weapons were now being used by wayward men to rob the Kalinga of their few possessions. With thousands of pesos on board for our payroll and our jeepney stuffed with gear and supplies, we were ripe for holduppers. I pondered the possibilities of being robbed or careening off the side of a slippery road. Lacking any evidence that the brakes and steering of our vehicle had been inspected, that the bridges we crossed were built to some government standard, or that the police occasionally passed

Departing for the Pasil River Valley, home of the Kalinga Ethnoarchaeological Project. (James Skibo)

our way, I opted for fatalism. I prefer to believe I have control over my life, but as we inched up the path I realized my fate was not in my hands. With new found freedom, I relaxed my death grip on the lashings and sat tall like a great, white hood ornament.

After many hours, our jeepney groaned to a stop high above the Pasil River Valley. The remainder of the journey would be by foot. Meeting our jeepney were Miriam Stark, Brian Trostel, and about thirty excited children. Miriam, Brian, Chris Turner, and several other members of the project had already been there for six months, since the end of the previous summer. I had seen slides and photos of the Pasil Valley, but had not captured the spectacular panorama I now had from the cliff overlooking Dangtalan, home base for the Kalinga Project. Amid the trees I could see the Dangtalan houses, many with smoke curling from under the roof edges. The hillsides surrounding the village were terraced with small, family-owned rice fields. Out of sight on the far side of Dangtalan, the Pasil River ran swiftly in a deep gorge, its course betrayed by rising vapor.

We unloaded the jeepney quickly, and the assistants and the thirty children carried the supplies and my duffels down the steep

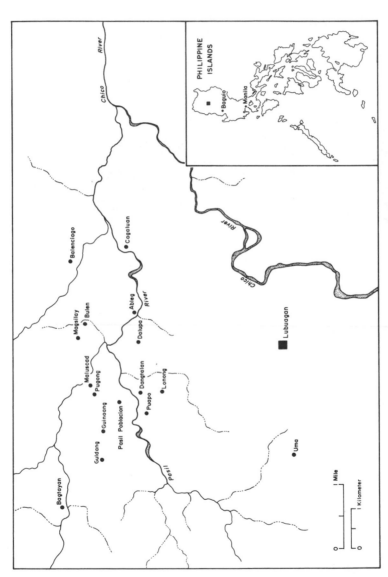

The Kalinga villages in the Pasil River Valley. (Reprinted by permission of William Longacre)

Two views of Dangtalan from the north side of the Pasil River Valley. (Reprinted by permission of the Arizona State Museum, William Longacre photo)

Family owned rice terraces irrigated by springs farther up the mountain. The small structure is a rice granary. (Reprinted by permission of the Arizona State Museum, William Longacre photo)

trail to their village. I was grateful for the porters because the trail was steep and a recent rain had made it slick. Though I was an experienced mountain hiker, this was certainly a challenge as I frequently found myself sliding several feet more for every few steps forward. By the time we arrived at the base of the cliff and the terrace just outside of Dangtalan, the first Kalinga children had already reached the village and announced our arrival. Between the first two houses at the edge of the village we were mobbed. Pushing our way through this crowd of laughing children and chattering adults eager to see the new Americans, I felt like a rock star entering the stadium for my next gig. Miriam, Brian, and Bill, having gone through this before, seemed to be enjoying it more the second time around. They announced our names and fielded various questions about us. "Where are they going to stay? What are they going to do?" Miriam told them that my name was "James Skibo." I heard my name ripple through the mob, "James Eskibo," a variation that stuck with me throughout my stay.

We came to Bill's house, which would serve as my home for the next week. I had no real responsibilities during this first week except to get acclimated prior to embarking on my own research. At that time, his house was one of the nicest in Dangtalan and was owned by a wealthy family (by local standards) who lived elsewhere. It was known as the "anthropologists' house" because Bill had stayed there during the 1975–76 research, as had other visiting anthropologists over the years. Most Americans probably do not know nor have they ever met an anthropologist, and I still find it amusing that the 300 Dangtalan residents had gotten to know so many bearded and bespectacled scientists.

The excitement of our arrival continued well into the night. Bill's house was large by Dangtalan standards, but it was certainly not meant to hold the thirty or more people now wedged in shoulder to shoulder. Those who could not fit in the house stood at the windows or door. Bill then pulled out a quantity of Ginebra San Miguel, the cheap, bottled alcohol preferred by the Kalinga. I was introduced to the Kalinga style of drinking, known to me during my undergraduate days as "doing shots." The project's male Kalinga assistants, plus members of our crew, drank several bottles of this colorless stuff, which came in a clear glass soda-pop bottle. Helpfully, the label said the contents were gin, because I would have never known from the taste. Gathered in a circle, tin cup and bottle in the center, each person took a turn throwing down a shot. The Kalinga were especially humored when Miriam took a shot, since this was not typically a female pastime.

The next morning, head throbbing, I explored the village. Dangtalan had about fifty dwellings in an area smaller than a football field. Houses were small, usually not more than fifteen feet square, and placed very close together, but a main passageway through the village helped to ensure a sense of openness. The houses sat on short stilts, giving each home a two-story look. The upper level provided people a dry living space, while the lower level was a refuge for chickens, pigs, and dogs. Wealthier families had house walls made of plank, but more often walls were of woven bamboo. The traditional roof style was grass thatch, but many homeowners had replaced it with metal. In the simpler homes there was just one room; larger dwellings had at least two rooms—a kitchen and a living room/bedroom. The floors of the houses were covered with bamboo strips lashed together with string and supported by cross-members spaced about four feet apart. To replace or clean the floor surface one simply had to roll it up and carry it out. Each kitchen was dominated by a hearth, a slightly raised square platform about three feet on a side. People cooked meals over an open fire in pots resting on three ceramic or stone supports. I was surprised to see that smoke did not fill the houses; it simply rose and flowed through gaps near the roof ends without choking the residents.

That morning I also toured the Dangtalan "facilities," which were constructed for the project and were quite elegant by Kalinga standards. Bill's assistants had rigged up a shower, sink, and separate toilet area. I was very impressed. Previous anthropologists in the village had not enjoyed such luxury. Bill cheerily informed me, however, that such an elaborate setup would not be available in Guina-ang, my site, a village across the river and a morning's walk from Dangtalan.

During much of my week-long residence in Dangtalan I focused on learning how to diagnose and treat some of the more

Village of Dangtalan. Houses are built with woven bamboo walls and either grass or corrugated metal roofs. Note the pots drying on the porch just to the right of the children in the lower photo. (Reprinted by permission of the Arizona State Museum, William Longacre photo)

Raised hearths in Kalinga homes. The rack above the hearth is for drying firewood. (Reprinted by permission of the Arizona State Museum, William Longacre photo)

Pouring coffee. (Reprinted by permission of the Arizona State Museum, William Longacre photo)

common ailments afflicting the villagers. A project such as ours had a responsibility not only to perform research but also to return something to the community. What the Kalinga desired most from us was simple medical aid. So Bill's house also served as the local clinic and apothecary. The people of Guina-ang would expect the same medical service from me, and I received an accelerated course. As it turned out, my role as health-care provider would be a much greater responsibility than I anticipated.

CHAPTER 2

Funerals Are Fun

THE WEEK IN DANGTALAN was soon over and it was time to begin research in Guina-ang. As I gazed from Bill's porch at the score of people there to carry our supplies and the dozens of others who could never get enough of watching the crazy anthropologists, I experienced another rush of self-importance. At that moment I could easily perceive how rock stars, athletes, or politicians, responding to an adoring crowd, are seduced by the emotional high. Power may be the most desired and abused substance of all, and I was not immune. This would not be the last time I fantasized about wiring for my meager savings, building a big house, buying lots of rice fields, and becoming a powerful Kalinga man.

Yet whenever I felt the euphoria of self-importance creeping into my spirit I needed only look at Bill to return to reality. I might have been considered an important man among the Kalinga, however unjustifiably, but I was just a mortal—Bill was the one with god-like status. Since the 1970s he had become one of the biggest employers, medical providers, and benefactors in the Pasil Valley. The Kalinga adored him. Anyone with money could gain a measure of status among the Kalinga; Bill was also admired because he respected their culture and never once tried to impose his ways on them. When I walked down a steep, slippery trail, I was left free to slide and tumble. But Bill, coming down the same trail, would be surrounded by spotters. If Bill could keep this in perspective, so could I. As he has said to me many times since, "I'm just little Billy Longacre from the U.P." And at that point my status among the Kalinga was solely as a friend of Billy Longacre. I drew comfort knowing he would be hiking with us to Guina-ang that day.

The first leg of our journey required a crossing of the Pasil. A narrow suspension bridge with metal cables now served the people of the area, having replaced the rope version about ten years earlier. Nonetheless, with the roaring river a hundred feet below visible through missing and rotting floorboards, travel across the 200–foot span hardly seemed an improvement. As we all piled on, it was no comfort to see each Kalinga man bounding across, effortlessly covering spaces once occupied by boards and placing his foot where he knew the wood remained solid. No one missed a step as the bridge bounced and swayed. I was careful to tread on the same spot as the person ahead of me, knowing that I was probably the heaviest person ever to have crossed. Bill had done so many times, but I did not think he counted; his spotters would have snatched him before he plunged into the raging waters.

Safely across, we began another ascent. Dangtalan was near the bottom of the valley and Guina-ang near the top, so most of the journey was an arduous uphill climb on a narrow trail. We quickly gained the north side of the valley, again with tremendous panoramic views of the Cordillera Mountains. Of course the Kalinga, having known nothing other than this view for their entire lives, took it for granted. Approaching the village, the trail suddenly widened to become a small road cut into the side of the mountain. We were now walking on a portion of the Spanish trail, which the Kalinga had long ago appropriated. The Spanish trail was originally intended to facilitate passage on horseback, but without horses or wagons the Kalinga preferred the shortest and fastest footpaths, not necessarily the easiest. This trail, once traveled by Spanish conquistadors, also was the escape route for Filipino nationalist and first president, Emilio Aguinaldo.

Prior to the arrival of the Americans in 1898, Aguinaldo led a fight to oust the Spanish, who had controlled the archipelago since Ferdinand Magellan landed on the island of Samar in 1521. One of Magellan's ships, the *Victoria*, eventually made it back to Spain and became the first ship to circumnavigate the globe, but Magellan himself was not so fortunate. He did not make it past the Philippine island of Cebu. Soon after Magellan claimed the islands for

Walking bridge over the Pasil River from the Dangtalan side. (James Skibo)

The Pasil River Valley and the Cordillera Mountains. The village of Dangtalan lies just above the bluff. (James Skibo)

the Spanish crown, he involved himself in local disputes and was killed in a battle with chief Lapulapu. Many of Magellan's men were also massacred by the islanders, but this did not deter the Spanish. Ruy Lopez de Villalobos in 1542 named the archipelago "Felipinas" in honor of Philip, the Spanish crown prince.

Although there were many lasting effects of Spanish rule (for example, the Philippines is the only Christian nation in Asia), Spain's grip on her colony was eroding by the late nineteenth century. It is at this point that the Philippines and the United States began their long and sometimes stormy relationship. Guina-ang and this very Spanish trail played a small part in that relationship. Aguinaldo and his army stayed for a time in the Pasil Valley and passed through Guina-ang while fleeing American soldiers after the outbreak of the Philippine-American War.

The United States acquired the Philippines through a series of miscommunications and blunders at the end of the Spanish-American War. Most of the war played out in the Americas, but a brief naval encounter in Manila Bay was pivotal in Philippine history. On May 1, 1898, Commodore George Dewey's squadron of nine ships entered the harbor and demolished a small, aging Spanish fleet. Soon after, Filipino nationalists led by Aguinaldo surrounded Manila and held the Spanish within the famous Intramuros, or Walled City. The Spanish situation was hopeless. With Dewey controlling the harbor and Aguinaldo's army surrounding the city, Spanish surrender was imminent. The original purpose of Dewey's incursion was to prevent the Spanish fleet from joining the fighting underway in Cuba. But President William McKinley, notorious for his indecisiveness, could not even locate the Philippines on a map.

McKinley's reluctance to act was also the result of poor communication between the Philippines and Washington (Dewey cut the cable between Manila and China, so McKinley did not even hear about the victory until almost a week later) and because the United States was divided over the idea of imperialism. Each side of the debate acquired famous advocates: the imperialists were led by Theodore Roosevelt, and Henry Cabot Lodge; while the leading anti-imperialists were former President Grover Cleveland, Mark Twain, and Andrew Carnegie. The Americans waffled and Aguinaldo took the initiative and declared Philippine independence from Spain on June 12, 1898. McKinley finally dispatched troops but still without a clear purpose.

The difficult communications between Manila and Washington gave Dewey and other U.S. military leaders enormous power to implement policy. One of their first orders of business was to enlist the support of Aguinaldo and the Filipino insurgents. American negotiators pledged, without authority, that the United States would honor Philippine independence. Even as American troops arrived in the Philippines, Aguinaldo was convinced they would only act as allies in driving out the Spanish. Aguinaldo, a well-traveled and educated man, had read the U.S. constitution and knew there was no authority to acquire colonies. After the surrender of Spain, Aguinaldo still believed that the Philippines would gain its independence despite the continued American military presence. McKinley, however, finally made a decision—to acquire and hold the Philippines. Aguinaldo prepared for war.

Mark Twain, then vice-president of the Anti-Imperialist League, declared in late 1900 to a New York City crowd that "we started

The Spanish-built Intramuros, or Walled City, with contemporary buildings of Manila in the background. (James Skibo)

out to set those poor Filipinos free too, and why, why, why that most righteous purpose of ours has apparently miscarried I sup pose I never shall know." McKinley thought to avoid conflict in the Philippines but the tensions were high between the two armies encamped side by side outside Manila. An American enlisted man fired the first shot that led to a war that killed many Americans and up to 200,000 Filipinos, many of them civilians. After a number of defeats, Aguinaldo and a following of about 250 soldiers escaped into the mountains of Luzon. It was at this time that Aguinaldo made the arduous journey through the land of the Kalinga with American soldiers hot on his trail. Aguinaldo was first pursued by Major General Henry Lawton, who was already famous for his role in the capture of Geronimo. Lawton, however, was denied further military fame in the Philippines by a sniper's bullet, and Brigadier General Frederick Funston took up the pursuit of Aguinaldo, eventually capturing him on the Pacific coast of Luzon in 1901.

As we trudged the last mile to Guina-ang, inadvertently retracing part of Aguinaldo's journey, I was anxious to see my new home. The entry into the village was actually quite different from

Dangtalan, where it had been necessary to wind our way through flooded rice fields. Guina-ang sat atop a wooded hill overlooking the valley, and the only rice fields were far below the trail. Rounding the final curve, we suddenly heard the murmur of village sounds. I could see houses through the trees and brush. The last of the Spanish trail, now wide enough for two horsemen riding abreast, was lined with blooming red bougainvillea, which made a stunning passageway into the village.

Our group snaked single file through the village, slowly gathering children. Compared to our arrival in Dangtalan, however, there was less laughing and chattering; most people just stood up from whatever they were doing and stared. Guina-ang was the oldest and largest village in the Pasil region. The hill on which the village was located had been terraced, like rice fields, to make flat areas for about a hundred houses. On first impression it seemed less compact than Dangtalan, and the houses were larger.

Yet 500 people lived here, plus countless dogs, pigs, chickens, and ducks. One might think the animals alone would turn the village into a smelly barnyard, every step fraught with danger, but the grounds surrounding each house were remarkably clean. The dogs, chickens, and especially pigs scavenged all household trash and leftover food, even the human and animal waste. The pigs, fully deserving their reputation, even took care of the dog droppings. The only weak link in this efficient cycle was the pig waste, which was usually swept up by young girls and dumped off the escarpment. Each household policed pig waste and other accumulated debris in its immediate vicinity. Despite the fact that Guina-ang was in a tropical rain forest and rain was a near-daily occurrence (belying the label "dry season"), little grass or vegetation grew on the dark, ripe-smelling, compacted ground. Banana, coconut, and other varieties of trees were abundant, but constant activity prevented even the hardiest weeds from taking root.

At the center of Guina-ang, we met our new landlords, Solono and Pasquela, who owned a larger-than-average two-room house. Masashi and I were to live in their bedroom, and Solono, Pasquela and their four children would spend the next four months living in their kitchen. The majority of houses in the village had just one

Guina-ang from the trail to Guldang. The village consists of about a hundred tightly packed houses and 500 people. (James Skibo)

room, so this arrangement was not unusual. The two rooms were divided by a covered porch, which the landlords quickly made into our kitchen by constructing a hearth and sealing off the entry to their side with a hastily woven bamboo wall.

Because we arrived in the village around midday, most of the adults were off working in their rice fields. But certainly all the children, their care givers, and finally most of the elderly began to crowd around, striving for a look. We retreated to our living quarters, the twelve-foot-square room we would share for a time, to remove ourselves from the mob and determine what to do next. Bill's capable assistants from Dangtalan, now seasoned veterans in dealing with the crazy anthropologists, handled most of the important camp logistics. They stored our food and supplies, organized the completion of the kitchen and bathroom, known throughout the Philippines as a comfort room or C.R. In our case the C.R. was little more than a hole in the ground surrounded by four walls. Our assistants also enlightened the curious Guina-ang residents regarding life with the strangers. While the assistants were unsure exactly what we would be doing, I am sure that they quieted the fears of the Guina-ang people by telling them what the project members had been up to in Dangtalan.

Our immediate task that day was to hire people to aid us in our research, and to do laundry, cook, and clean. Many people sought these jobs but competence was essential, especially in our research assistants, as we would be unable to acquire language proficiency in just a few months. In Dangtalan, Bill had found success hiring female school teachers because their English was quite good and they were generally respected members of the community. But the two college-trained teachers in Guina-ang were teaching at the village school and unavailable for other work. Roberto, Miriam's landlord in Dalupa and an unsuccessful candidate for district mayor, had accompanied us to Guina-ang to facilitate the hiring. According to Bill, the primary reason for his help was to repay some campaign debts by urging us to hire people from families he owed favors. Though it was probably not the ideal way to hire workers, we did hire his selections for cook and clothes washer (which meant someone to beat our clothes on a rock). But ability alone would determine our selections for research assistants, and we let it be known that we would interview anyone who could speak English.

Quickly, a line formed and our interviews began. I truly hated the process. Most of the interviewees were so nervous that their English skills failed them and they could not even look at us. I now felt quite the colonial overseer—an uncomfortable sensation for me. We struggled to find a better way to hire our helpers. Luckily, Roberto, Bill's primary assistant for the previous fifteen years (not the mayoral candidate), arrived in Guina-ang later that day. He did a quick screening of candidates, and we relied heavily on his opinions. We hired Nancy, the local midwife; Julia, the district mayor's college-educated daughter; and Edita, who was also trained as a midwife. Because we would be studying pottery, a woman's technology, our female assistants would be responsible for collecting much of our data. We also hired two male assistants, Amboy and Joseph, to be our travel companions, to deal with the daily logistical problems and, as it turned out, to be our friends.

In the midst of hiring assistants, we received invitations to about a half dozen different houses for *marianda*, which is usually a mid-

Our landlord, Solono, weaves strips of bamboo to make walls for our bathroom. (James Skibo)

afternoon snack. In each house we ate a sweet, sticky rice, *chaycot*, and drank tepid coffee so saturated with sugar that it made my teeth ache. The Kalinga grew their own coffee, which was delicious, but I could never get accustomed to the lukewarm, syrupy consistency they favored. It took me weeks to convince them I preferred coffee without sugar, which they considered unhealthful if not insane. Late that afternoon, Solono treated us to a meal of boiled pig, butchered in our honor just outside our house. By that time, people were returning from the day's work, and they milled around gossiping and discussing our intentions.

Darkness came too quickly. On most days the setting sun signaled the end of work, but since Bill would be leaving us in the morning we lit the petromax gas lanterns and continued to discuss research plans. With the only light in the village shining through the open windows, our house looked like a single, bright Christmas ornament. A couple dozen children still mingled outside trying to get a glimpse. So many had climbed a tree to stare into our open window that it curved to the ground. The sight reminded me of how a swarm of bees, following their queen, will light upon a branch and bend it from their combined weight.

Several hours after sunset we turned off the petromax to get some sleep; it had been a hectic day and we were all exhausted. But a half hour later there was a rap on our door. I opened it and saw that most of the village had assembled around a fire in the plaza. The man asked us to come out. I looked at Bill and he told us that it was now our village and project and that Masashi and I needed to go without him. Before our arrival, Bill had told us the story of how fifteen years earlier he had faced a similar fireside council in the village of Dangtalan. In that original meeting, Bill explained his intentions and fielded questions from the villagers. This had occurred in the early 1970s, soon after the first moon landing, and he was asked questions such as how he *really* knew that Americans had landed on the moon. Bill thought his meeting was going well, but a recent translation of an audio tape made that night revealed a great deal of uncertainty about the project and some distrust of Bill. In a heated debate that was not translated for Bill at the time, one Kalinga man stated that Bill was planning to take their pots and sell them for a big profit, while another man was heard to say that he suspected Bill intended to take the Kalinga potters to America and make the women slaves.

I experienced some anxiety as we walked onto the porch and could see the subdued faces of the Kalinga *pangat* illuminated by the flickering fire. Masashi, Brian (also in Guina-ang for the night), and I were directed to sit on a log on the inner ring. After a lengthy pause, one elder rose and made a short speech. Although an older man skilled in English sat next to us as translator, he provided just one or two words from every paragraph of the speech. Consequently, I did not get much of the content of the admirable, though seemingly angry, presentation. My translator's occasional words assured me that all was going well, but from the speaker's body language and intonations I would have guessed otherwise. Not only do the faces of the Kalinga, even when relaxed, have the appearance of an angry scowl, but their spoken language, especially in a public forum, is choppy and aggressive.

The first speaker relinquished the floor as a second man stood and launched into another oration. The Kalinga admire a great speech and invariably the most influential men are skilled orators.

Every elder possessed oratorical skills that would make a televangelist envious. The average American is unskilled and unpracticed at public presentations and usually does poorly when there is an occasion to speak. But the Kalinga are frequent public speakers and performers and relish an opportunity to demonstrate their skill.

Through my sporadic translation it appeared that the discussion involved the positive and negative aspects of our presence, which until then was only gathered as gossip through Bill's assistants and other Dangtalan residents. After sitting quietly through several speeches, Brian, now a veteran Kalinga ethnographer, decided it was time to say something and volunteered for the task. Brian could not approach the proud Kalinga oratorical style, but he did a good job explaining our intentions in English. He said that we had traveled all the way from Arizona in America to live with and learn about the people of Guina-ang. He told them we would be providing free medicine to show our appreciation. Nearly every older Kalinga man can speak or at least understand English, a by-product of Word War II when the countryside was overrun by American soldiers and teachers after the Japanese were evicted, so Brian's words were understood by the *pangat* and his speech seemed well received. Following several more Kalinga speeches, an elder stood and directed his speech directly at me, first speaking in Kalinga and then in English. "We do not make pots here," he said sheepishly, "but there is one old woman who made them when she was young. We will tell her to make you pots." Many heads nodded in agreement.

This was the first of many misunderstandings, the frustrating aspect of living in Guina-ang and doing something very alien among its people. In this case at least it was easy to see the source of confusion. The research in Dangtalan and Dalupa, both pottery-producing villages, had focused on the potters and the process of pottery distribution. Our research, however, was to focus on pottery *use*, so we selected a village without potters; they obtained their pots from Dangtalan and Dalupa. I found myself standing, convinced that it was now time to make my own speech to clarify our purposes.

I started by saying how happy we were to be in Guina-ang and how warm and generous everyone had been on our first day. I said that there was no need to tell the woman to make pots because we were not interested in pottery making. I told them that we wanted to watch people use pots in their houses: cooking, eating, and cleaning. The Kalinga *pangat* nodded their heads in understanding and seemed relieved they would not disappoint us by their lack of village potters. I then went on to describe the specifics of our research and what they could expect to happen. I said that we wanted to visit all one hundred houses and look at all their pots. We wanted to count them, measure them, and ask the women where and when each vessel was bought. I thought that the house inventory was one area that might meet some resistance because it seemed a bit intrusive, but again they nodded their heads in agreement.

If I had to select a single factor that led to the ultimate success of the pottery use-alteration study, it would be the cooperation of the people and their grant of complete access. My goal was to develop a comprehensive understanding of the relationship between how vessels were used and the resultant use-traces. To accomplish this goal successfully, I needed unhindered access to their homes to observe pots being used. All ethnographic projects that I am aware of encounter resistance at some point and some village members who prefer not to cooperate. But never did we encounter anyone in Guina-ang who was not happy to spend a morning with us as we removed from their shelves every one of twenty or more pots and severely interrupted their day. Would most Americans let a stranger arrive unannounced and rummage through their kitchen? But the Guina-ang Kalinga knew Bill (if only indirectly) and thus we were not utter strangers. This complete access makes the Kalinga Project data unique. I finished my speech by saying that we also wanted to spend an entire day in selected houses watching people use their vessels. Before I sat down I asked them if these intrusions would be acceptable.

The Kalinga now had a better idea what I planned to do, yet they were unsure why it mattered. For archaeologists who study pottery, the significance of such a study would have been clear: archaeologists need methods to better understand how pottery vessels are used. At the time of the project, archaeologists could make only very general connections between vessel design and functions such as storage, processing, cooking, or transport. The questions being asked by archaeologists, however, required more accurate statements about vessel function; analysts wanted to know what was being stored, processed, cooked, or transported and what activities were involved in these various pottery-use behaviors.

Use-wear analysis of stone tools had become commonplace in archaeology by the 1980s, but nothing comparable had been done with ceramics. A Russian archaeologist, Sergei Semenov, was the first to demonstrate that specific stone-tool uses leave microscopic traces on the edges and can be linked to function. For example, cutting bone, flesh, plant material, leather, and scraping hide, shaping wood, and carving bone all leave different micro-chip patterns on the tool edge. Today, stone-tool analysts look at both the micro-chips and the polish on the tool edge to develop more detailed accounts of prehistoric stone-tool use behavior.

What I hoped to accomplish among the Kalinga was something analogous to a stone use-wear analysis. Pottery, of course, is quite different from stone tools in the types of use activities and the resultant traces. I had observed on prehistoric pottery three types of use-alteration traces: abrasion, carbonization, and residue. Abrasions are the scratches and nicks that occur on the relatively soft earthenware pottery. Carbonization is caused by sooting from a cooking fire on the exterior and by the burning of food on the interior. Residue is the remnant of the vessel's contents, absorbed and trapped inside the pot's wall. While these traces occur frequently in prehistoric pottery, it was nearly impossible to provide accurate links to specific activities. In stone-tool use-wear analysis, researchers performed experiments in which they cut, drilled, and scraped various materials with replicas and then observed the resultant traces. This was also possible with pottery and had been done somewhat earlier, but with the Kalinga project we could observe actual pottery-use activities and then study the used vessels to determine abrasion, carbonization, and residue patterns. Very few places remained in the world where this could be accomplished.

As I stood there confidently explaining what I wanted to do, I really had no idea whether it would turn out. Original research always begins with great optimism, and it often ends with results that are less than satisfactory. Would I be able to collect the necessary data in Guina-ang? Would my observations of pottery use be sufficient? Would the used pots taken back to Tucson have tell-tale traces that would permit me to connect them to vessel use? I asked myself these questions daily.

The fireside plaza discussion continued for another hour. At times we were asked specific questions, but it became clear that our stay was favored. Finally, a wrinkled old fellow stood to speak. He said that his people appreciated the medicine and that we could stay. He concluded by announcing that every house in Guina-ang would be available to us for our research. This was the old man, too old to work in the fields, whom I had seen for most of the day quietly observing us as he cared for his grandchildren, one small child tied to his back. I was surprised to learn that this fellow commanded such power in Guina-ang. In the States, a man of his age, too weak for demanding physical labor, would probably no longer be contributing directly to the community. If he had led what is considered a successful life in America, he would most likely own a condo in Florida and spend his mornings fishing and his afternoons golfing. But among the Kalinga, the years of acquired wisdom and experience are not wasted—it is the oldest males who command the most respect and authority.

Next day, Bill, Brian, and the Dangtalan entourage departed Guina-ang, leaving Masashi and me to work out the kinks of research and village life. I walked Bill to the end of our village. By the time I returned to our house a line of people seeking medical attention had formed on our porch. With our assistants working as translators, we began to poke bellies (as they say in the medical profession). This became one of the most trying and time-consuming—yet rewarding—aspects of my stay. I was amazed to see what basic medication could do for bodies unaccustomed to such treatments.

One of the most common maladies was arthritis, especially among older women. Our neighbor lady had a bad case, her hands and feet increasingly deformed. Some days she could barely walk, but after two aspirin she was transformed. Soon after treating her I would see her outside sweeping and bounding up and down her steps, which earlier in the day were an obstacle. As she smiled at me

I saw the attraction of a career in medicine; it was indeed a pleasure to make people feel better.

Other common complaints were simple colds or infections. In the Philippines one could buy virtually any drug without a prescription and we had a variety of antibiotics. People would come in with a hand or foot swollen to twice its size from an infection that might have started as a simple cut. Usually a course of antibiotics was all it took to restore them. But the most common request by the villagers was to treat *colong*, or intestinal worms. Although the people scrupulously cleaned their plazas of animal fecal matter, which harbors the eggs of the worm, many people, especially children, couldn't avoid the same worm that infested their pigs and dogs. Someone with *colong* generally manifests no overt symptoms, but most villagers were determined to flush their bodies of the invader. Dispensing the medicine (called T.M.Z.) on a daily basis, I was curious why the Kalinga seemed so upset about a harmless pest until one day about six months later when I was back in Tucson.

A luxury I appreciated fully only after my return to the States was that of a toilet seat and the privacy of a morning constitutional. But enjoyment turned to horror one morning as I stared into the porcelain bowl at a ten-inch-long white worm. "*Colong!*" I yelled, though in a low, throaty sort of way. I cannot imagine when a scream from a bathroom is ever a good sign, and this was certainly the case on that memorable Tucson morning. I now had a belated appreciation for the Kalinga concerns. I called a doctor and related my problem, how I acquired worms, and how easy it was to treat in the Philippines. The drug was called T.M.Z., I explained, and with one dose the Kalinga expelled these intestinal demons. He told me he had never heard of the drug and that he had never treated anyone with worms. He would get back to me. I ground my teeth at the thought of my physician, in his foothills clinic with the padded armchairs and an aquarium, having a good laugh on the phone with his doctor buddies trying to figure out a way to treat worms. Not confident that my physician would be much help, I asked Bill that day at the university if anyone had brought back some T.M.Z., or if he knew more about the drug. Although he had none of the drug or any real information, he appreciated my problems. He now has a wonderful story to tell—which he does on a regular basis, usually at a nice restaurant with people I am trying to impress.

But my physician called the next day quite excited about his little research project and the possibility of treating an ailment other than earaches in whiny kids. He told me that the worms usually live in pairs and medical treatment was necessary to remove the worm's partner. He then asked me if I had saved the worm. I could not even reply. The only approved drug for generalized treatment of these parasites required five straight days of treatment. "Impossible," I said. "We just need T.M.Z., a tiny white pill that you take once and that has no side effects." He told me that the drug is not available in the United States.

So I went to the pharmacy and picked up a bottle of pills with a dosage calculated on my body weight—after all, it was only the worm that they wanted to kill. I was supposed to take the medication for five days, but after three days of nausea, not eating, and the smell of poison and death emanating from my body, I had success: the *colong* spouse was terminated and expelled.

The tradition of providing medicine to the Guina-ang residents may have been started by an American family that lived in Guina-ang for a number of years. The man was a member of the Summer Institute of Linguistics and his wife was a nurse. The mission of the Institute is curious to me; all over the Philippines and in many other countries of the world the missionaries record local languages and translate the Bible into local dialects. They don't preach, baptize, or otherwise try to gain converts, they just translate the Bible. Inadvertently, this is a tremendous service to anthropologists and linguists because to translate the Bible the Institute people must study the language intensively, then create a grammar. They probably believe that having a Bible in a people's native tongue will produce converts, but among the Kalinga I would estimate that no one became a Christian as a result. Most Guina-ang residents, in fact, considered themselves as having been Christian for generations.

The Summer Institute linguist did translate one chapter of the Bible into Kalinga. Several Guina-ang residents had copies as curiosities. At least a third of the town, including most of the young people, were literate and could read both English and Tagalog (the national language), but Kalinga is only a spoken language. Of course the residents of Guina-ang did appreciate the medical care provided by the missionaries. I sometimes wished I had the benefit of medical training, like the Summer Institute nurse, because I soon began to encounter problems well beyond my abilities.

During our first week in Guina-ang, one of my assistants brought me to the house of a middle-aged woman who had been suffering a high fever for several days. When I entered she sat up with a struggle. Her faced contorted with pain as she answered a couple of my questions translated through my Kalinga assistants. The affliction was especially serious, my assistants told me, because her husband had been too ill to work for many years, making her the only household member able to labor in the fields. I touched the side of her face and was appalled by the heat of her skin. I asked my assistants if they thought she had malaria—my only experience with the disease was limited to seeing it in movies. They said that it indeed looked like malaria. Although the insect that carries malaria does not live in the Pasil Valley, it is found in the lowlands and the disease is especially prevalent in Tabuk. I asked her family if she had been to Tabuk lately. They said she had.

There is an effective cure for malaria today but it was very expensive by Kalinga standards, requiring a three-day stay in the Tabuk hospital at a cost of about 400 pesos (the average daily salary in the Philippines was then about 25–30 pesos). Most Kalinga, however, have little or no cash. The currency exchange rate at the time of our stay was quite favorable to U.S. visitors—400 pesos was about $20.00. Earlier Bill had informed us that we might encounter situations where hospital treatment was necessary. In those cases we were to rely on our own judgment and money. I told the lady and her family that I would pay for the hospital stay and malaria treatment and asked my assistants to arrange for transport.

Transport of the ill or dead was done by the young men of the village. From the time males were teenagers until they married, they lived together in a separate house with primary responsibility for the defense of the village. A secondary responsibility was to serve as the "ambulance." A number of these young men were summoned to the malaria victim's bedside and they quickly constructed a stretcher from bamboo poles and blankets. They strapped her in snugly, put the stretcher on their shoulders, and began without complaint the tortuous two-hour walk to Ableg and the nearest road. There they put her on a jeepney for the journey to Tabuk.

Two weeks later she appeared on my porch with a huge smile on her face. She could speak no English but words were not necessary as she raised her arms up and spun around as if to say "look at me." That was the best twenty bucks I have ever spent.

During my stay I sent another person to the hospital for malaria treatment, this time a man about my age whom I had befriended. I also provided medical funds for a woman with a broken arm and for a baby running a high fever. I derived great satisfaction from returning something of value to the people who were being so generous with us. But there was one instance, late one night, when my offer to pay for medical treatment was refused.

By about halfway through my stay it was common for my assistants and other young men—approximately my age mates—to come to my house for conversation and sometimes some drinking and singing. I enjoyed these times immensely. We learned a lot about each other in these informal sessions and I soon considered these men my friends. One night as Amboy, my primary male assistant, was trying to teach me a Kalinga song, a man and his teenage daughter walked into the house. His daughter looked pale and her hand was wrapped with a cloth. Her father said she cut herself with a *bolo*, the ubiquitous machete used for all cutting needs, while slicing vegetables. I began unwrapping the blood-drenched cloth as Amboy looked on curiously. When I pulled the cloth off, the tip of her finger came with it. Her knees buckled immediately. Amboy and her father caught her limp body as I held her hand and arm. Amboy gently laid the unconscious girl on the floor, which gave me an opportunity to look at her finger more closely. The cut was on the meaty front of the finger, although part of her nail had also been severed. The tip of the finger was hanging by some skin and I could see the bone, very white even in the dim candlelight. It was fortunate that she fainted for I could manipulate her finger without her cringing and moaning.

Losing consciousness is an interesting response to pain. Perhaps it is this reflex that permitted surgery in prehistory. One of the most intriguing archaeological finds is evidence for the practice of trephination, a crude form of brain surgery that involves cutting out a piece of the skull. We have evidence of more than 1,000 cases of trephination, probably performed to reduce cranial pressure due to skull fracture or to alleviate headaches. Remarkably, over half the skulls had healed, meaning the patients survived the procedure. Possibly their patients, like this young girl, simply lost consciousness, which permitted the ancient surgeons, wielding stone knives, to perform their surgery without the aid of anesthesia. I thought that like the prehistoric surgeons, I might work on this girl's finger as she lay motionless.

I gently placed the tip of her finger back in place, cleaned the wound as well as I could, and then wrapped it tightly to stop the bleeding. After I stopped pushing and pulling on her finger she began to regain consciousness. The Kalinga, both men and women, are extremely tough people and highly resistant to pain. This girl was no exception. She woke up, said a few words to her father, but did not cry or complain. She still was quite pale, so I allowed her to remain on the floor for a while as I addressed her father.

"I think she needs stitches," I said. "The doctor can sew the piece back in place and it might be OK." Amboy translated my advice, but her father said she did not need to see a doctor. "Tell him I think it might get infected," I said to Amboy, "and that I will pay for the trip and the treatment." This was again translated, but I could tell that he was having a hard time convincing the man. Amboy became very animated as he gestured several times at the girl's throbbing finger. Finally, Amboy, with an astonished smirk on his face, turned back to me and said that the father would not let her go to the doctor. The father said that he had seen much worse cuts than that and no doctor was necessary. I was stunned. Suddenly I felt the need for malpractice insurance. I told the father that I would come by in the morning and if the finger was infected she really should go to the doctor.

The next morning Amboy and I went to their house with gauze, tape, and antibiotic salve. The young girl met us and looked much better than the previous night. I began to remove the bulky finger wrap that I had hastily applied twelve hours earlier, but the girl raised her hand for me to stop. She lay down on the floor, face down, and stuck her finger in the air—this time she would be ready if she fainted. Amboy smiled and poked me in the ribs. I removed the wrapping, being much more careful when I reached the final layer. The finger, though caked in blood, looked remarkably well. I rinsed it with rubbing alcohol, applied some salve, and wrapped it tightly again. I returned the next two mornings and the wound remained infection-free. Within two weeks she did not even need to wrap the finger. I guess the father was right.

Even with the best of medical care, people do eventually die. During the first six weeks of my stay, four people died in Guina-ang or the nearby villages of Malucsod or Pagong. Thankfully, I had not administered any medicine to those folks. But four funerals in such a short time seemed a bit excessive, and I hoped the Kalinga would not think I had brought bad luck. The problem with funerals, from the cold and unfeeling perspective of doing science, was that they interfered with my research. Kalinga funerals were several-day affairs that my assistants needed to attend. I was hoping to avoid the funerals outside of Guina-ang, but by the day of each occasion my assistants had convinced me that I needed to go to Pagong or Malucsad as well.

My first experience with these affairs began one night when I was shocked out of a sound sleep by a piercing wail. It was not a scream nor was it crying, it was a sound I had never heard before. Until then I thought all this talk about the hair on someone's neck standing up was not something physiological but just an expression. But as I heard the lonely howl echo through the sleeping village, I can honestly say the hair on my neck did stand up. I reached back and felt it. I was not the only person startled from sleep, for soon I heard the murmur of voices. A ritual wailing around the time of death by relatives is common throughout the world, and after my neck hair had gone limp again, I surmised that a Guina-ang resident had expired. The wailing continued, but I soon went back to sleep and was only wakened by my watch alarm at the now customary time of 5:00 A.M., ready for another day of recording household vessel use.

I stumbled in the dark to the house I would be visiting for the day (I was now recording pottery vessel use for the entire day, which unfortunately meant arriving at a house before the morning meal was prepared). It was still quite dark in the house, with the only light coming from a homemade oil lamp. But as usual the household members—already up and about—seemed quite pleased to see me. The woman of the house did not have any matches, so she asked her son to run next door for an ember to start the fire. Soon the fire was going and the woman, while preparing the meal, was carrying on an animated conversation with her neighbor, who was in her own kitchen doing the same. I guessed that they were discussing last night's wailing, so I asked who died. She told me the name of an older woman whom I had never met. Yet the village chattering was at a higher pitch than usual, and I suspected this would not be a normal day.

Despite my initial annoyance about the loss of precious research time, the four funerals turned out to be remarkable and, in their own way, even enjoyable. I usually attended only the feast days when a carabao was butchered, many pots of rice cooked, and several large vessels of local wine consumed. Like American funerals, Kalinga death ceremonies are costly. At least one carabao had to be butchered, and families would often go into debt to bury a loved one. But there the similarities between American and Kalinga funerals ended.

The first noticeable difference was that the funerals were almost joyful if the deceased was elderly. It was a party, especially for the men who congregated by the dozens in shade near the deceased person's house to drink wine, tell stories, and sing songs. I enjoyed having a Y chromosome at this point because most of the women sat in the house with the corpse and took turns wailing. The houses were extremely hot and the women wedged shoulder-to-shoulder. Men, except for next of kin, were not permitted in the house, but I was invited in because the family wanted a picture of the deceased and I had a camera. I found this to be an unusual request but I

Hard at work. (Becky Skibo)

complied. Having no pictures of the person while living, they wanted to have a "remembrance." Interestingly, this practice was also common in nineteenth-century rural America.

At the beginning of the twentieth century, American funeral homes became more popular as a way to relieve grieving families of the logistics associated with a family death. Previously, the family, just like the Kalinga, prepared the body and displayed it in the parlor, whose wall would be lined with photographs of other deceased family members. At about this time, the *Ladies Home Journal* suggested to its readers that the parlor, no longer functioning directly in the death ritual, should now be called the "living room," which we still use. The advent of funeral homes brought an end to the parlor display of corpses and the custom of photographic death remembrances.

The deceased Kalinga woman was dressed in traditional clothing, adorned with necklaces and heavy gold hoop earrings that distended the woman's ear lobes. On entry, I saw the deceased sitting, strapped to a newly fashioned bamboo chair. A close relative sat next to the corpse shooing away flies with a home-made swatter—a short stick with leaves attached to the end. The women wedged together even tighter to make room for me, and I watched solemnly as relatives took their turn next to the corpse for more wailing. I sat on the floor for a while in the cramped quarters and dutifully used my camera for several shots of the body, which I promised to give the family after the film was developed. It was near noon and Kalinga houses, especially those with the new metal roofs, could get very hot. But this house, only about twelve feet square and packed with as many as twenty women, was unbearable. Happily, my gender allowed me to escape to the party just outside.

The first order of business was butchering the carabao. I grew up in a rural area and had seen cows, pigs, and chickens butchered, but I still cringed at the manner of this gentle animal's demise. Several men held the animal's head up and with a sharpened *bolo* another man opened its main artery with a swift blow to the throat. Immediately blood gushed out and men rushed to collect it for use in cooking the entrails. From my front-row seat I watched the animal die slowly, its heart pumping blood into the waiting receptacles. Unfortunately, these were not pottery vessels.

Several men then started the long butchering process. All of the animal, including the skin and head, were consumed here or divided into portions for consumption later. The men worked for hours cutting the meat into small chunks that were then attached to bamboo sticks and distributed. Roughly a quarter pound of meat was given to all present based upon their status; the close relatives and *pangat* received the better pieces. This was one of those occasions where I sincerely enjoyed my relatively high status because I received two nice hunks of lean meat. The alternative was to receive a lower leg and hoof or some undetermined entrails. With a diet that consisted mostly of rice and vegetables I enjoyed this little treat.

The funerals did in fact provide an opportunity to observe pottery use at village-wide gatherings. Every Kalinga household had ten or more large cooking pots that that they took down only to cook for large gatherings such as funerals, weddings, or the occasional house moving in which a group of men actually disassembled an entire house and carried it to a new location. While I was interested primarily in daily pottery use, these larger gatherings were

Butchered carabao. In the foreground are pieces of meat on the end of bamboo rods to be taken home by the guests. (James Skibo, photographer)

notable because I got to see a whole different set of pots in use. The same basic food was cooked, but what caught my attention was that most of these vessels were quite old, passed from mother to daughter. This was significant because most of the everyday ware lasted a year or less. Many of the "ceremonial" vessels could last generations since they usually were stored in house rafters out of harm's way. Cooking pots break often because of thermal shock: the heat difference between the interior and exterior of the vessel is so great that it creates tremendous stresses. Initially this only causes small cracks but eventually it results in the failure of the pot.

One of the most common misconceptions by archaeologists about prehistoric cooking pots is that appearance is everything. Cooking pots, referred to in the trade as "crudware," are often low-fired with a rough texture and large amounts of temper—nonclay material such as crushed stone—that all ceramics must have to survive drying and firing. What we have learned recently is that the elements that make an ugly pot are part of what makes it a wonderful cooking vessel.

When I ask my archaeology students to make a pot out of clay, everyone can make some type of vessel—making a ceramic pot is not very difficult. Making a cooking pot, however, is very difficult. If I were to fire the student-made pots, allow them to cool, then place them over a heat source, all would probably shatter because of their low thermal-shock resistance. Prehistoric potters, worldwide, discovered that by adding lots of temper, texturing the exterior surface, and keeping the firing temperature low, they could make a vessel with higher thermal shock resistance, one that would survive the tortures of fire. A vessel might look ugly to you and me, but to people waiting for their food to cook it would be a thing of beauty.

The temporary hearths set up around the Guina-ang plaza for the funeral had cooking fires with temperatures around 600 degrees C, while the interior of the large pots never exceeded 100 degrees C. Without high thermal-shock resistance, the valuable food would have spilled onto the ground between the pieces of broken pot.

After consuming some of the funeral carabao, which involved eating the small boiled pieces served with their own juices in a coconut-shell bowl, the drinking, singing, and story-telling began. The family of the deceased also had to purchase a number of large vessels filled with *basi*, the locally made sugar-cane wine. Usually there were only about six or seven drinking cups available, so the approximately forty men would proceed in rotation. Each received a coffee-mug-sized portion of wine to be downed quickly. The wine was very sweet and filled with pieces of sugar cane, swallowing which could be avoided by straining the wine through one's teeth. The lack of cups insured a decent interval between drinks and nobody got very drunk. After several rounds, however, I knew that I could no longer serve as designated driver. The men of high status sitting in the inner circle received more, and, as I glanced into the eyes of the *pangat* sitting next to me, I realized he too was feeling no pain.

No Kalinga gathering goes without speeches. After everyone had several glasses of wine, men began standing one at a time to praise the deceased. A new jar of *basi* was opened, but unlike the biblical story the best wine was not served last. This batch of wine was somewhat bitter and the men commented on its merit like Napa Valley wine tasters. The mayor of Pasil, the local school principal and a very intelligent and capable man, sat next to me. He described Kalinga funeral customs and provided an excellent translation of the speeches, which in most cases eulogized the deceased and described her good qualities as a mother and worker. But after a time the topics wandered; men didn't often get a public forum so they took the opportunity to discuss recent outbreaks of tribal war, community water problems, encounters with holduppers, and other events of import. The mayor then stood and gave a short speech ending in English. He said that it was good to have us as guests at the funeral and he then invited me to say a few words and to describe American funerals.

I stood and they gave me a cup of wine—customary for the speaker. I told them how happy I was to be there and that I was enjoying the funeral very much. I told them that most American funerals are quite sad with no laughing or joyful singing of the type I had seen that day. I was about to tell them how morticians suck the blood out of the corpses and replace it with embalming fluid, but I decided this sounded too barbaric and put me at risk of being killed as a witch. So instead I told them about my grandparents' funerals, my only experience with the American burial ritual.

This prompted a number of questions and a discussion comparing the relative merits of Kalinga and American funerals. Even though I left out the part about embalming, the consensus was that Kalinga funerals were better because theirs was a celebration, not a time of sadness, and that American funerals were deficient because people did not leave with a part of the butchered animal, as was proper. I agreed; through the eyes of the Kalinga, American funerals did seem a bit strange. Among the Kalinga, the closest relatives prepare the body for the funeral as a final gesture of love, whereas in the United States the bodies are whisked away and prepared by strangers as if unclean. Americans, like all peoples, tend to think of their customs as the natural way, the correct and proper method.

Reflecting on American customs through the eyes of others I was given a new awareness of the central anthropological concept of ethnocentrism and the related term "cultural relativity." Franz Boas, the father of American anthropology, introduced this notion as a reaction against the social Darwinist approach that permeated

Kalinga man (right, with glass of *basi*) gives a speech to the men assembled for a funeral. Women are gathered with the corpse in the house in background. (James Skibo)

the natural and social sciences in the late nineteenth century. At the time, some European and American scholars were busy applying Charles Darwin's teachings to contemporary human groups with the predictable result that nonwhite, non-European peoples were considered "less evolved"—a corruption that Darwin himself found annoying. Boas reacted strongly to these racist theories by introducing the concept of cultural relativity, which states that one cannot make judgments about the merits of one culture over another. Even the most bizarre behavior, according to Boas, must be understood within the context of that culture and without the baggage of one's own cultural biases.

One of the most dramatic demonstrations of cultural relativism is the practice of infanticide, which is the killing of one's baby. Infanticide was practiced by the native peoples of the Arctic and certain desert nomads and at face value is repulsive. But if you view this practice from the perspective of an Arctic hunter, it makes more sense. Population in a hunter-gatherer group must be controlled—too many people threaten the survival of the entire group. In the absence of birth-control methods these people had few alternatives.

Food preference is another area that can demonstrate cultural relativity and the related concept of ethnocentrism. Delicacies for some people are taboo for others. The Kalinga routinely eat dog, a practice that most Americans find abhorrent. In fact, virtually everything that we as Americans view as correct, right, and normal is culturally defined.

When the enthusiasm for speeches dwindled, the singing began. The first phase of the singing was done solo. Men stood one at a time and sang ballads that had a repeating chorus but featured original verses about the deceased composed on the spot. These songs were quite beautiful and I was impressed by the men's skill and passion. Certainly there was a range of talent, but even the least skilled gave impressive performances. While admiring the singers, I stared at the ground intently like a grade-school child without an answer. Luckily, I was temporarily spared the humiliation of a solo when the singing went into its final stage, village competition.

The competition consisted of groups of older men from every village singing a complicated song, which was sung only at funerals. Like the solos, each song had some original words, and the performance was judged by both the group's singing ability and the spontaneous lyrics. When it was time for them to sing, the Guina-ang men pulled me along to stand with their group. I had been listening carefully to the previous performers but I could not master the complicated tune. But with a few drinks now under my belt I stood arm in arm with my five Guina-ang compadres as if in an Irish pub and helped them belt out the requisite tune. The Kalinga seemed to appreciate my willingness to participate despite my obvious lack of talent.

CHAPTER 3

Once Were Headhunters

*The Kalingas are a fine lot of head-hunting savages,
physically magnificently developed, mentally acute,
but naturally wild.*

So WROTE DEAN C. WORCESTER, secretary of the interior for
the Philippine insular government, during the first part of the so-
called American Period, which lasted from 1898 to 1946. A
University of Michigan zoologist turned imperialist and government official, Worcester was appointed by President McKinley to
carry out duties that accorded with America's new role as colonial
power. Compared to standards set by other imperial powers, particularly Spain, the American occupation was humane. McKinley
ordered Worcester and other commission members to "exercise due
respect for all the ideals, customs, and institutions of the tribes
which compose the population, emphasizing upon all occasions
the just and beneficent intentions of the government of the United
States."

Despite the noble intentions, colonial rule remained an open
sore for the Filipinos who not only thought they were fully capable
of self-rule, but who lived with the fresh memory of bloody battles
with American soldiers that killed thousands of their countrymen.
The rancor is evident, for example, in a 1908 editorial in the Philippine paper, *El Renacimiento*, regarding Worcester.

But there is a man who, besides being an eagle, also has the characteristics of the vulture, the owl, and the vampire. He ascends the
mountains of Benguet ostensibly to classify and measure Igorot skulls,

to study and civilize the Igorots, but, at the same time, he also espies during his flight, with the keen eye of the bird of prey, where the large deposits of gold are, the real prey concealed in the lonely mountains, and then appropriates these all to himself afterward, thanks to the legal facilities he can make and unmake at will, always, however, redounding to his benefit.

That such criticism was even permitted represented an improvement on Spain's rule. Nonetheless, Worcester sued *El Renacimiento* (Spanish for "the rebirth") and its editors for libel, forcing the newspaper into bankruptcy. His legal victory did little to win Filipino hearts. The editor of *El Renacimiento*, Teodora Kalaw, received a stiff fine and a jail sentence (he was subsequently pardoned) but earned such popular support that he was elected to the Philippine assembly in 1909.

Reading Worcester's published writings, one can discern his dismay at the anticolonial sentiments both in the Philippines and at home, though he seems to have remained blind to the universal human need to reject overlords of any stripe. Regardless of the number of roads, bridges, or schools the Americans built, the period will always be resented by Filipinos and a puzzle for students of a U.S. constitution that explicitly forbids colonial occupation.

Yet Worcester was not totally oblivious to his surroundings. Drawing on his scientific training, he provided outsiders with one of the first descriptions of the Kalinga and other Mountain Province people during what he named the "Exploration of Non-Christian Territory." In order to draft legislation for the "control and civilization of numerous savage or barbarous peoples," he traveled deep into the rugged Kalinga homeland to collect firsthand information. Crossing a particularly difficult mountain peak, the rotund Worcester suffered temporary paralysis of the legs. He recovered with the aid of "stimulants" and was able to visit the Kalinga, a group that already had earned a reputation for aggressive and violent rejection of outsiders. When he entered his first Kalinga village, Worcester was met by 120 men brandishing head-axes. But Kalinga elders named Saking, Bakidan, and Bogauit served at different times as Worcester's guides through the territory and these respected men saved Worcester's party on this and other occasions.

In fact Worcester's group was traveling through the region during a time of intense Kalinga fighting. Several times they came upon villages that were in the process of celebrating successful head-hunting raids. The intrusion of outsiders during this period of heightened tension prompted a council of suspicious Kalinga *pangat* to rule that the white intruders should be killed. An armed and angry mob then surrounded Worcester's hut for an entire night hoping to carry out the sentence, but Bakidan told the villagers that they would have to kill him first. Bakidan and one of the mob leaders, each armed with head-axes and shields, actually dueled at one point during the night, but the angry group was eventually pacified and Worcester, though shaken, was permitted to move on.

The lasting images of the Kalinga provided by Worcester, graphically described in two *National Geographic* articles (complete with a photograph of a headless corpse), is that they were unfriendly, aggressive, war-like, xenophobic, and given to barbaric practices such as body tattooing and head-hunting. Were these descriptions of the Kalinga accurate? Were these the same people I was visiting, just two generations after Worcester?

Edward Dozier, a cultural anthropologist who lived and worked among the Kalinga in 1959 and 1960, offers a different view of the Kalinga. Dozier's descriptions are particularly telling because at the time of his visit there were still many Kalinga who had personally witnessed the 1905 Worcester expedition. Dozier states, "A more generous and hospitable people would be difficult to find." He goes on to say, "I frankly like the Kalinga," and after my visit I concur with this sentiment. Are the Kalinga friendly, cooperative, and loving, or aggressive, suspicious, and warlike? Could Worcester and Dozier both be correct? I believe so and can think of three reasons for the difference.

The first reason relates to the fieldwork methods and the situation between the Kalinga people and Dozier and Worcester. Worcester made a series of short trips into the mountains to collect information about tribal groups. Such brief encounters with the Kalinga and other peoples would have given Worcester only a superficial acquaintance. Dozier, however, was an experienced anthropologist.

To be basic, when anthropologists study a single group it is called "ethnography," an approach that requires investigation of all aspects of a culture, including head-hunting and raiding as well as family and village organization, foodways, marriage practices, and religion. Anthropology had learned long before Dozier that one can understand a culture only by participating in people's lives. Head-hunting may be disturbing to outsiders, but the anthropologist seeks to understand why it occurs in the context of that culture. In the eyes of the Kalinga and many people around the world, the practice of sucking blood out of corpses prior to burial (which we call embalming) might be as disturbing as head-hunting is to Americans.

A second factor that contributes to the great differences in the Kalinga descriptions arises from the differing reasons for Dozier's and Worcester's visits. Dozier's presence among the Kalinga was stimulated simply by anthropological curiosity. He wanted to learn about and then describe the lives of wet-rice cultivators living in the mountains of Luzon. He published his descriptions primarily in journals and books intended for other anthropologists and students. Worcester's agenda was to control and pacify the mountain people. The *National Geographic* articles emphasized the bizarre and "barbaric" practices of the Kalinga and enabled Worcester and the McKinley administration to justify to an uncertain American public policies intended to control, educate, and ultimately "civilize" the tribal groups of the mountains and all of the Philippine people. Full-page photos of bare-chested women, half-naked men, filed teeth, and headless corpses were silent but powerful persuaders.

Finally, profound changes among the Kalinga had taken place between the visits by Worcester and Dozier. Because of greater opportunities for travel and inter-regional trade, the Kalinga instituted the *bodong*, or peace pact, which reduced hostilities between rival groups. From a purely anthropological perspective, the peace pact is one of the most fascinating aspects of Kalinga society. One of Dozier's most important books about the Kalinga, *Mountain Arbiters*, reflects the more recent emphasis on negotiating regional disputes and creating a system of custom law that serves as an alternative to the blood feud. Kalinga men now gained regional distinction and high status through skill in arbitration, not by collecting trophy heads.

The *bodong*, which means "bound together," arose early in the American Period, though colonial intervention cannot be credited. Kalinga *pangat* created the system simply by expanding and formalizing a system of adjudication already in place to deal with kin or village disputes. All peoples of the world have systems to deal with murder, theft, and other crimes against individuals, but the Kalinga formalized their system to an unprecedented degree. During my stay, there were dozens of peace pacts clearly establishing conduct in inter-regional contacts and procedures to be taken for any crime from murder, rape, and theft, to courting a married woman, or simply being inhospitable.

Each *bodong* was a document, in English, kept in the home of the peace-pact holder. The first negotiators and peace-pact holders were the most feared and respected head-hunters, but today they are often the wealthiest and most respected men or women in the community. Solono, our landlord, was a peace-pact holder, an honorable position but with heavy responsibility. The punishment for murder, for example, was quite specific: life taken was to be paid by life. The peace-pact holder had to carry out the sentence, meaning he might be required to kill one of his own kinsmen. This was infrequent, however, perhaps because murder was often the reason for the breakdown of a particular peace-pact. It was more common for a peace-pact holder to wound a kinsman as punishment for a nonlethal but violent crime against an individual from another region.

The peace pacts reduced the amount of intergroup raiding and effectively ended the practice of removing people's heads, but the blood feud continues and murder was still common. Inter-regional hostilities heightened just after our departure from the Philippines and continue today to the degree that our study could not presently be continued. Now with guns instead of head axes, Kalinga men still seek vengeance for the death of a relative. The *bodong* does not ensure an absence of hostilities, but it does serve as a deterrent and a means to adjudicate infractions should they occur.

One of the first things I noticed about the people was physical stature. Short-statured (the average man is approximately five feet six inches in height), the Kalinga are slim and strong. Midwest America, where I grew up and now live, is known as the home for the largest percentage of overweight Americans. Too much beer, cheese, and fatty foods, and too little physical activity have led to a population that supports many cardiologists specializing in heart-bypass surgery. The Kalinga were a contrast to the people of my homeland. Although the Kalinga have their own assortment of lifestyle-related ailments, heart disease would not have been one of them. Most Kalinga men I saw could have starred in television commercials for exercise equipment. A good diet, dominated by whole-grain rice and vegetables, plus continuous exercise and good genetics, made for an almost ideal physique. Just walking to and from their fields each day was the equivalent to at least an hour on a stairmaster, the popular piece of exercise equipment in Western health clubs. Moreover, every woman spent some time each day wielding a five-foot-long pestle to pound rice and vegetables. The rhythmic thump, thump, thump is a sound that can be heard all day long in a Kalinga village. Gathering firewood, clearing fields, building terraces, and carrying large loads are tasks that fill the days of most Kalinga from the time they are ten years old.

I was also shocked by the lack of obvious signs of aging in Kalinga men. Older Kalinga men were with me often because they are the village decision makers and the ones responsible for the activities and well-being of an outsider. I was impressed by the absence among them of gray hair, receding hairlines, or frail bodies. The exact age of the men was unknown but they were all old enough to have learned English in the World War II era. This would have made them at least sixty years old at the time. The women, on the other hand, were not often blessed with a comfortable and healthy old age. Post-menopausal women seemed to age rapidly and were afflicted by arthritis. I was often shocked on meeting my older informants' wives, who in some cases could have passed for their mothers. While I am uncertain of the specific causes, it was undoubtedly related to the fact that women there had as many as ten children, no mean feat in any part of the world.

The Kalinga people were generous and warm, and Dean Worcester and I do share one common experience among them that vividly

Pounding rice with large wooden mortars and pestles. (Reprinted by permission of the Arizona State Museum, William Longacre photo)

Preparing a rice field for planting. The woman in the photo has a goiter on the right side of her neck, an enlargement of the thyroid gland and a common affliction among the Kalinga. (Reprinted by permission of the Arizona State Museum, William Longacre photo)

A woman wearing a hat and banana-leaf sun shawl weeds her rice field. (James Skibo)

Harvesting rice. (James Skibo)

Cutting into a hill to prepare a new house site. (James Skibo)

demonstrates the weight they placed on friendship and loyalty—their willingness to lay down their lives for a friend's protection. Bakidan and other influential Kalinga men befriended Worcester and thus were committed to his well-being. All members of the recent Kalinga project were afforded the same level of loyalty and friendship. The Guina-ang Kalinga told me many times that as their guest I was covered by their peace pacts and protected by their village. It moved me when a Kalinga man said with cold sincerity, "We would die to protect you," though I felt it might be a bit much to ask of someone I hadn't known very long. In common with most Americans, I would lay down my life to protect spouse and children, but would I do the same for a neighbor or a house guest? Probably not, nor would my American house guest expect me to do so. Still, given my vulnerability in Guina-ang, I gladly accepted their vow of protection while hoping there would not be an opportunity to test it.

Working and living in the Kalinga village brought me in daily contact with most segments of the community. My research focused on pottery, so I spent much of each day with women, the makers and users of this technology. I also worked closely with the

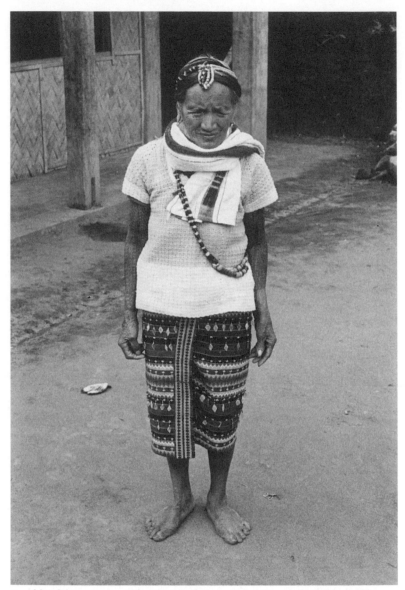

An old Kalinga woman with cataracts that cause her eyes to be light-sensitive. The tattoos on her arms are a now-defunct sign of high status. (Reprinted by permission of the Arizona State Museum, William Longacre photo)

male Kalinga elders, the local power brokers who protected—and monitored—their American guest. And the children, curious about their new and strange-looking neighbor, were my constant companions, especially early in my stay. But I was unable to interact with my age mates, the young men of the village. Unfortunately this was also the only group that held me in a certain amount of suspicion.

Young Kalinga men (from age fifteen to late twenties) were a complex mix of contrasting traits. On first impression they were tough, mean, and quick tempered—true macho men. It was the side of Kalinga men that Worcester saw. These were warriors, the people called upon by their kin to kill someone in another village to avenge a death and to protect their village. Although killings as a result of blood feud have been reduced, regional aggression is still common and it is the young men who bear primary responsibility. Even today, young unmarried men sleep together in a house on the village edge and guard against intruders.

Because of his short visit, Worcester did not find that the Kalinga men are also gentle, warm, affectionate, and kind. In some ways Kalinga men have mastered what is asked of the modern American man: tough but gentle, stoic yet expressive. American men struggle with these contradictions while the Kalinga moved between extremes with ease. After being in the village for some time I would see the same macho and threatening man playing tenderly with a baby or walking arm-in-arm with another Kalinga man. I was fascinated by the contrast and sought to learn more about it. But I also wanted to become a part of their group simply for my own benefit—I wanted the friendships. Living in a foreign land can be lonely, and I wanted to become closer to people of my own age and gender.

Loneliness and alienation are among the most common problems of ethnographic fieldwork, given that one is living among people who do not share one's language, food, or customs. In the worst possible situation, a fieldworker might be distrusted and even disliked by community members, and an almost total sense of alienation could seriously jeopardize a project. We were treated well among the Kalinga—one could not have asked for a better situation—but feelings of loneliness and despair occasionally did arise.

Luckily, because my stay was relatively short and I kept extremely busy, I experienced only short bouts of depression.

Perhaps the most vivid description of the emotional ups and downs of ethnographic fieldwork comes from Bronislaw Malinowski's personal diaries. Every anthropology student reads Malinowski's works because he was one of the founders of social anthropology. In addition, he helped refine the field methods that anthropologists have used to this day. His most famous ethnographic work took place among the Trobriand Islanders and other Polynesian peoples. His published diaries, originally written in Polish, sample thirteen months of fieldwork undertaken between 1914 and 1918.

This small representation was published in 1967 by Malinowski's widow, Valetta, well after his death in 1942. The journals were never meant to be read by *anyone*; thus they are a raw portrayal of his innermost thoughts. Some readers cringe when the famous anthropologist discusses his sexual fantasies and his occasional hostility toward the people he was studying, but I find the unsanitized view of his life during fieldwork refreshing. The daily entries remind me a little bit of a Woody Allen character in that during his daily self-analysis he obsesses about health, sex, and his various inadequacies. Many students of anthropology have taken heart that even the great Malinowski was haunted by thoughts that his research methods were inappropriate or that his work might be irrelevant. And any male can take heart that even one of the most influential social scientists of the twentieth century spent more than just a little time on impure thoughts.

But the predominant theme in Malinowski's journals is his loneliness. In his words, "Occasionally in the afternoon—violent fit of dejection; my loneliness weighs upon me." One way that he dealt with depression and loneliness was by reading novels—also a common means of escape for the members of the Kalinga Project. Malinowski periodically took his novel reading to dysfunctional levels, however, sometimes spending days glued to a book, not even stopping during meals. Often, after such binges, he would vow in his journal never to do so again.

I never experienced loneliness to the degree described by Malinowski, yet his research had one advantage over mine in that he could, if he desired, have daily contact with virtually any aspect of Trobriand society. I studied only pottery and therefore spent most of each day among women. If I were female, this would have been an opportunity to develop close relationships, and when I was not collecting data I could have joined with them while they pounded rice, worked in their fields, or carried out domestic chores. Almost all of these activities were done in groups, and there was a delightful banter between the women that certainly made such mundane tasks bearable. But it would have been inappropriate if not dangerous for me to participate beyond the bounds I had described to the *pangat*. It was obvious that if I wanted to participate more in Kalinga life and develop friendships I would have to be accepted by the local equivalent of my peers.

I began a campaign that slowly bore fruit. First, I worked to convince the young men that I was not a competitor for female attention. Prior to Becky's arrival, I proudly displayed her picture and deflected certain forms of female interest. Despite my overt demonstration of marital ties, it was suggested to me that I could take a mistress—common for high-status Kalinga men. Although fieldworkers seek to participate as completely as possible in the life of their host community, romantic involvements are generally the exception. Even if I had been single, a liaison would easily have threatened my stay in Guina-ang. Spending nearly every day, all day, with the wives and daughters of the community was potentially fertile ground for misinterpretation. The least suspicion that I was flirting with women instead of studying their pottery would have caused tremendous tension. Moreover, Bill Longacre likely would have put me on a slow boat back to Tucson for jeopardizing the entire project. Of course the young Kalinga men did not know of my commitments to proper fieldwork behavior and marital fidelity. Here I could not simply announce my disinterest in a Kalinga lover, I had to demonstrate it. This did not take long, however, because my behavior was ceaselessly observed and discussed by the villagers.

The principal village informants were my female assistants. Our pottery research required female assistants, and we had hired married and mature women. Besides being a crack research team, they were also very effective at informing people, including the young men, about the work and my deportment. My assistants, hence the entire village, also learned a good deal about Becky to the extent that she was almost a cult figure by the time she arrived. Within several weeks the young men were satisfied that I was not a threat, and a major barrier was overcome.

A second part of my strategy to befriend my male age mates was to hire two of them as assistants. Amboy and Joseph were young men with standing in the community. I paid them a weekly salary like my female assistants but they collected little if any data. Instead they served as guides and protectors when we traveled outside the village, and they were available as translators and problem solvers, helping me deal with the incessant problems of village life. They also were my companions when I was not collecting data and provided entry into the men's world. Paying someone to be a friend is equivalent to wearing a pork chop around your neck so the dog will play with you, but I did it shamelessly. They probably learned as much or more about me as I did about them and passed this intelligence along, furthering my efforts to connect with the masculine side of village life. I also enjoyed their company tremendously.

Basketball, now a universal sport, provided the third key to better acquaintance with the men. Guina-ang had a small dirt court constructed by the Belgian Catholic missionaries who were still active in the Kalinga region. I love basketball and even now try to play several times a week as part of a faculty noon basketball group, an activity common to nearly every American college campus. I had seen the basketball court immediately, but it was usually being employed to dry rice. Initially I concluded it was just an unsuccessful aspect of the Belgians' proselytizing efforts. But basketball is extremely popular throughout the Philippines and, I soon discovered, among the Kalinga.

One afternoon I was drawn to the court by the familiar but unexpected sound of a bouncing basketball. Two boys were shooting baskets for pesos. Each would put a peso on the ground and then shoot from that spot; the one making the basket kept the money. I wondered where these young hustlers got the money,

Amboy(r), Joseph (l), and I, along the Pasil River, dressed in our best clothes and searching for a party, which we never found. (James Skibo)

since it was relatively scarce in the village, but I couldn't resist trying my luck. Not wanting to take their money, I intended to throw the game if necessary. I need not have worried. The youngsters were quite accurate, and my pockets were soon empty.

Several days later, I again heard the sound of a bouncing ball, but this time a group of older boys and young men had assembled. I was delighted to find out that during the dry season they often played late-afternoon games, and I quickly worked basketball into my daily schedule. After hunching next to the hearth all day long in a hot, smoky kitchen, the exercise was wonderful. Moreover, I learned a whole new style of basketball.

In common with the American game, there were two hoops (about six inches lower than standard), five people per team, and the same general characteristics—dribble, pass, and shoot. But that is where the similarities ended. The men played with ferocious enthusiasm, barefoot or wearing rubber flip-flops. Most were six inches shorter than I, and I led off thinking it would be like playing junior-high kids. That was another mistaken assumption because all the players turned out to be strong, quick, and aggressive. If I had been cut down to their height, I would have suffered broken bones, yet despite crushing collisions and numerous flips to the hard ground I never heard a complaint. And although my mutant size made me stick out on the court like Shaquille O'Neal, I never had to hold back for fear of hurting someone.

It took just one day of participation for me to sense that the final barrier between the young men and me had started to crumble. There is something magical about the effects of intense physical activity. Whether climbing a mountain, chopping wood together, or banging bodies on a basketball court, the physical exertion and effort toward a common goal can create bonds that are unattainable any other way. When Kareem Abdul Jabbar, the all-time leading NBA scorer, finally retired, someone asked him what he would miss most about the game. His reply was that he was going to miss the guys in the locker room. Cheering crowds, money, and adulation did not compare to the friendships that developed in the course of his athletic career. Perhaps the persistence of the Kalinga blood feud or even the warlike nature of humans everywhere can be explained as a need to bond under conditions of intense physical effort. The Belgian priests may have been on the right track in trying to institute basketball as a substitute for deadlier activities.

Amboy and Joseph often came to my house after dark, when basketball concluded, to talk and sample the local gin. Amboy mentioned to me that some of the other young men would like to join us but were a bit shy because their English was not good. (English was taught in the grade school but most were not fluent.) I told Amboy he should invite them to our get-togethers. I made sure I had plenty of Ginebra San Miguel plus a good supply of cigarettes (Kalinga men smoke with a passion); my evenings were soon devoted to these booze-and-bull sessions. Typically, we sat in a circle on the floor, the young men with their arms linked in some fashion. Out came the gin, one of the guests removed the crimped metal cap with his teeth, the bottle made its rounds, and soon we were all singing, talking, and telling stories. I enjoyed these sessions tremendously, even though my lungs ached from the smoke, and the daily hangover made the 5 A.M. start to my research even more challenging.

My impromptu men's club became a village fixture until Joseph informed me that several *pangat* were concerned about the excessive drinking. I asked Joseph what I should do, and he suggested that I limit our drinking parties to several times per week. Actually, reducing the frequency of these sessions was something of a relief, since I certainly did not want to contribute to youthful corruption, but I was concerned it might jeopardize the relationships that I enjoyed and had worked hard to develop. Again I needn't have worried. It was as if we all had gotten in trouble together and had been admonished by our elders. At that point I was a member of the young men's group.

Basketball, drinking parties, and a shared reprimand were small things, but they bespoke universal aspects of the human condition that transcended our obvious and outward differences. Below the surface, the Kalinga were not much different from my neighbors in Alpha, the small, Upper Peninsula town of my boyhood. Guina-ang and Alpha were roughly the same size. If one had morning coffee at someone's house in either village one likely talked about the weather, gardens, problems with children, recent trips, or neighbors. But like Dean Worcester, I was sometimes as guilty as anyone of relying on superficials and concentrating on differences. When I came to Guina-ang, I had a hard time telling people apart because I focused on physical traits alone. Ironically, many Kalinga people told me that when we first arrived they found it difficult to differentiate some of the project members. "All Americans look alike," they often told me. Many people initially called me Brian, the name of my blond co-worker—I had dark hair and a beard.

Despite the many worldwide differences in the way people speak, eat, and practice religion, and in their skin color, and body shape, today I am awed by human universals. For one thing, we are a single species, capable of mating and producing viable offspring. In our planet's history, however, this was not always the case. The brutish-looking Neanderthal—a subspecies of modern humans— seems to have lived in proximity with anatomically modern humans for thousands of years, but recent DNA studies have shown fairly conclusively that Neanderthals and humans share very little genetic material. Much earlier, about 2.5 million years ago, *Homo habilis*, the world's first toolmaker, lived in East Africa with other hominid species that, unlike *Homo habilis*, became evolutionary dead ends. Our times are unique in the world's history as only one species of humans or human-like species exists. Thus, the many cross-cultural similarities should not be surprising. A well-known anthropologist, George Peter Murdock, once tabulated a list of cultural universals that included religion, courtship, joking, medicine, tool making, surgery, music, marriage, law, games, family, education, dream interpretation, and many more. From an evolutionary perspective, these human similarities seem to support the idea that all people in the world share genetic material from only 200,000 years ago—our 10,000th great-grandmother.

This is still a controversial theory in paleoanthropology—a specialty that studies human origins and evolution—but there is something inviting about it. Sometimes called the "Eve Hypothesis," it promotes the idea that every person on this planet shares genetic material from one woman who lived and died about 200,000 years ago. That does not mean that there was only one woman at the time, only that by chance we all carry this particular woman's genetic material. The people who support this theory are not the stereotypical researchers pondering fossil remains in dusty museums, rather they are molecular geneticists studying mitochondrial DNA in the sterile confines of the laboratory.

We inherit DNA in the cell's mitochondria (which produce energy) only from our mothers, so by studying DNA these researchers can establish lineages of living people related maternally. Mitochondrial DNA mutates rapidly, and, according to these researchers, can serve as a clock to track human evolution. For example, molecular geneticists have found that black Africans have the oldest DNA, confirmation that the first several million years of human evolution took place in Africa. Quite literally, we may all be related.

While the world's people do share a great-grandmother somewhere in their ancestry, whether 200,000 or 2 million years ago, no one can deny the existence of human variation—which is one of the attractions of anthropology. On the flip-side of human universals we get to explore the grand sweep of human diversity.

To understand the culture of a particular people and their similarities and differences in relation to other peoples, anthropologists often try to go back as far as possible. The Kalinga are no exception. The Philippines consist of a group of islands, separated from the continent of Asia by the South China Sea. Students often ask me how people got to these places without the capability for ocean travel. The first Filipinos got to the islands in the same way that the original Americans arrived, they walked.

The climatic history of the world is characterized by alternating periods of warm and cold. During cold eras, or ice ages, the world's temperature drops, glaciers advance from the poles, and the global environment changes dramatically. For example, during the last episode, the Wisconsin Glaciation, which ended just 11,000 years ago, the deserts of the American Southwest were temperate grass and woodlands, and central Illinois, where I now live, was covered by an ice mass perhaps several miles thick. There have been twenty glaciations at fairly regular intervals in the last 2 million years. We are about due for another. Global warming will be no match for the powers of the next ice age.

One of the remarkable aspects of the glacial periods is that ocean levels drop significantly. There is a finite amount of water on our globe, and when so much of it is locked up as ice there is simply less of it in the hydrologic cycle. During the last glaciation sea level dropped by 300 feet, dramatically altering coastlines. Britain was connected to mainland Europe; North America was connected to northern Asia, and the Philippine Islands were connected to mainland Asia.

In 1891, Eugene Dubois found a skullcap near the village of Trinil in central Java. The fossilized bone was human-like, but Dubois believed, correctly, that it was from an archaic human species. He named it *Pithecanthropus erectus*. We now know it as *Homo erectus*, the first species in our evolutionary line to travel out of Africa; make fire; produce a comparatively sophisticated stone tool, the hand axe; and perfect the art of big-game hunting. Recent research has placed *Homo erectus* on mainland Asia as early as 1.7 to 1.5 million years ago. If so, *Homo erectus* lived through some bitter ice ages. It would have been possible for this ancient type of human to travel to the Philippines at a period of low sea level, though there is no evidence for an arrival. In the Cagayan Valley on the island of Luzon, very near the Kalinga homeland, there have been claims for *Homo erectus* tools, but it seems these finds are false. Although the excavations revealed plants from the Middle Pleistocene (during the era of *Homo erectus*), the associated stone implements have been shown to originate from a much more recent occupation.

At this writing, the best dates for human arrival in the Philippines come from Tabon Cave on the island of Palawan. There, in the lowest levels of the cave, archaeologists have found stone tools and human remains dated to between 28,000 and 22,000 B.C. These were anatomically modern humans who walked there during a particularly cold period. By 6000 B.C. the Philippines were again islands, and the environment was similar to that of today. This does not mean the islands were cut off from other populations, for the peoples of Southeast Asia and the Pacific quickly developed the means and skills for seafaring. Thus the Philippines were first occupied by big-game hunters during the last ice age, but since then there has been continued immigration and a very complex history.

While it has not been proven conclusively, there is general agreement that the Kalinga homeland was unoccupied until about 500 years ago. The current consensus is that the Kalinga moved into the upper reaches of the Cordillera Mountains at the beginning of the Spanish Period, possibly to escape colonial oppression. It is probable that they moved into the region in village or even family groups. Yet at no time in their recent history were the Kalinga a unified people, despite a common language. In fact, the name "Kalinga" was given to them during the American Period by Governor Hale in 1907 as an administrative move. He drew the label from *kallinga*, meaning "constant warfare."

Theories about human universals are one thing, but it was my relationship with Amboy that took me from the high-flown language of textbooks to a real understanding of human commonality. As I struggled to find able assistants in my first few days in Guina-ang, many of the villagers told me about Amboy. When I asked to meet him, they said he was in the mountains digging for gold. The Cordillera Mountains have gold deposits near the surface, and some young Kalinga men, especially those who had not inherited rice fields, would try their luck as wildcatters. The work is dirty and dangerous. No one ever struck it rich, but most found enough gold for basic support of their families. Injuries were frequent because mining technique simply meant burrowing into a hillside hoping to hit an ore vein. Some of the men had worked previously in the Batangbuhay gold mine, which operated for a number of years until regional unrest shut it down. Its only vestiges were an occasional hard-hat and a Pasil River now devoid of life from arsenic, a gold-processing byproduct.

I met Amboy's wife, who had recently given birth to a girl, and she indicated word of our interest would be sent. Proving the effectiveness of word-of-mouth overland communication, Amboy appeared in a couple of days. As soon as I met him I knew he was unique. Unlike most of the would-be assistants, Amboy was confident and unintimidated. His English was as good as anyone's in the village, including the schoolteacher's, and certainly better than others of his age group. I hired him immediately. He turned out to be one of the most talented people I have ever known.

Besides being intelligent, charming, and witty, Amboy was gifted musically and athletically. He had a beautiful voice in a village of great singers, and he knew hundreds of songs—Kalinga, Tagalog, and English. In that regard, I was indeed a disappointment to him and other young men as they were hoping I could teach them more American songs. They actually knew many more than I did. Amboy could pick up a beaten guitar with a missing string and snap off American ballads by the dozen. I was in awe. Assuming that I would be expert in all things American, one night Amboy demanded, "Sing us an American love song." Like most college students, I was up on the popular music of the day and figured I could come up with a song or two. After several false starts I found I could summon a lot of snippets but not a single, complete, American love song. Elvis would not have been proud, and the Kalinga men were puzzled too. Later, after Amboy finally gave up on learning new American love songs from me, he carried the nights, which the other men enjoyed as much as I. He did teach me two Kalinga *salidomays*, and I still can sing them from start to finish, but only after consuming a fair amount of gin according to Kalinga custom.

Amboy was also the best athlete in the village. On the basketball court with many able competitors, he was not only faster and stronger but he possessed basketball skills that would have made him stand out anywhere. During our late-afternoon games Amboy's team usually won.

Still, Amboy's talents did not guarantee him success. Kalinga society, like American, commonly takes wealth as a measure of achievement, and Amboy was not a wealthy man. Wealth in Kalinga society most often means rice fields. Amboy was one of the youngest sons of a man with many sons and few rice fields, so he received no fields. He had married into one of the richest families in Guinaang, but his wife was the youngest daughter and thus was given only one small field at marriage. He lived in his father-in-law's house and made a meager living teasing bits of gold from the mountains. If the Kalinga had still been active head-hunters, Amboy's athleticism, leadership, and intelligence would have contributed to many successful raids and assured him a place of respect. But the old avenues to status were no longer available to modern Kalinga men. Instead, many young and talented Kalinga men and women went to college and become teachers and other professionals (for example, there is now a Kalinga lawyer, an anthropologist, and a dentist). I talked to Amboy several times about such opportunities, and he told me that he thought he was too old to begin such a journey.

Amboy had spent his time after high school, when his talented age mates were off at college, with the New Peoples Army. He never spoke of this experience, merely shaking his head in silence when I persisted. One of his high school teachers told me that Amboy was a bright student but frequently in trouble. I cannot help but feel guilty when I think of him now. His intellectual abilities and potential easily surpassed mine, yet I was the one seeking the advanced degree in science. This man might have been the most talented person in the Cordillera Mountains, but it was possible he would never attain any measure of status. Had we been swapped at birth, I would have been a poor Kalinga man with no rice fields and little standing, but what would have become of Amboy growing up in the middle-class American world? I like to think his multiple talents would have been recognized, nurtured, and developed, and his future might have been limitless. Anthropology, which understands the power of culture, has always taken the position that our environment largely determines our destiny, not our genetics. Having known Amboy makes me even more resolute in the belief that, biologically, we are all one species, but our environment determines our destiny.

I often think about Amboy and wonder what has happened to him. While I am not good at distant relationships, I have written him several times. Ironically, Amboy and I must also share this fault because my letters have gone unanswered.

CHAPTER 4

Ants for Breakfast

Every day I sat in a different house watching women cook and use their pottery. One morning, about a week after her arrival, Becky entered the house where I was carefully observing a woman prepare lunch. I had left at dawn with the advice that Becky could always find me by asking anyone in the village my whereabouts. Even if the person knew no English, Becky could simply ask, "Mr. James?" which is what the Guina-ang people had decided to call me. Doing so, she was quickly delivered to the one house in a hundred where I was visiting. It was a quick way to locate someone, but it was also suffocating and a bit like being in a fish bowl. Every action and every movement was soon common knowledge.

Walking around the village at first, I was trailed by a large giggle of children. For the youngest I may have been the first non-Kalinga and almost certainly the first American whom they had ever seen. They seemed particularly fascinated by my beard, or *eming* as they called it. Because Kalinga men have little facial hair, encountering a man with a beard must have been like seeing one with hair growing from his palms. Not only did I have hair sprouting from unusual places, but I was white and probably the palest, tallest man they had even seen. When I was a boy I would pay a quarter to see the Tall Man or the Werewolf at the carnival, but these kids got the thrill for free.

The Guina-ang children gradually lost interest in me, and I could walk the village unimpeded. Nonetheless, my activities continued to be the business of all and a never-failing topic for gossip. My mail, which was delivered to Guina-ang sporadically, was a common subject of discussion. By local standards, I received quite a lot, first from Becky and then from other family members and colleagues, rarely delivered by the same person. I am still unsure of the mail route, though it appears to have been handled by whoever happened to be traveling between villages. A letter or two might arrive in the hands of a man from Dalupa in Guina-ang to visit relatives, or the missionary priests might serve as carriers. Sometimes I was alerted hours before its actual delivery, or I would receive my mail at unusual times and places. One afternoon I was in a nearby village attending a funeral when a stranger came up and handed me several letters. This uniquely Kalinga system, seemingly haphazard and inefficient, was remarkably effective. I received all my correspondence safely and once it reached the Mountain Province it arrived promptly. My assistants often commented on the number of letters. All love letters, I told them, which the Kalinga, true romantics, readily appreciated.

The effectiveness of the gossip network was even plainer to me after a small event. One morning I stumbled, half asleep in the predawn light, up the steps of a house to perform my usual observations. I sat next to the hearth and watched the woman of the house prepare breakfast by the light of a cooking fire and a small, homemade oil candle. My routine was to take notes and ask simple questions, but on this morning, after a restless night's sleep, I could only manage to sit quietly and sip coffee waiting for the caffeine to pry me out of catalepsy. Her husband entered with a bamboo tube and emptied its contents into a large metal frying pan. I sat up straighter and took notice because I was studying their cooking and this was a new food for me. The low light made it impossible to see what it was, but the woman gave me the Kalinga name, *alaga*, which I dutifully recorded while she stirred the mystery meal. I knew I would get a better look at the food as it had become customary for me to eat three meals per day at each house I visited. Originally I tried to avoid this, but people seemed quite insulted when I even suggested that I return to my own house for meals. Moreover, the Kalinga had a custom of not killing a person once he or she had been fed, so I appreciated their offer.

Cooking was finally done and I received a generous portion of boiled rice, the staple at every meal. Then came the mystery food, piled in a steamy heap on my plate. The light was dim, so I put my face close to the plate for a look. I made out small black shapes and slightly larger white spots. Ants and ant eggs! Not wanting to insult my hosts, who had gone to great trouble, I took a good-sized spoonful, closed my eyes, and feigned delight. It may have helped that I was hungry, but the ants were rather tasty with a sort of vinegar-and-nut taste. Still, I could not get it out of my mind that I was eating insects. Knowing this was new for me, my hosts asked how I liked it. "*Mumpia!*" I said with enthusiasm. Delicious. Word spread immediately. As an honor, I was served ants and ant eggs in every house I visited for the next several weeks. Mercifully, ants went out of season but not without teaching me a lesson that I soon put to use.

As I walked the trails around Guina-ang I noticed a distinct lack of wildlife. It looked and smelled like a jungle that should have been teeming with animals, but I was met with stillness and silence that at times seemed almost eerie. Where were the chirping birds, the darting squirrels, or the occasional deer bounding across the trail? I asked about this, and the villagers told me that the old people talked about hunting deer long ago and that there were once many more wild animals, but they had all been killed. We often have a romantic view of traditional peoples living in harmony with their environment, but this is a notion that is far from reality. "You have to go farther up into the mountains to find deer today," an assistant told me. The Kalinga are a people hard up for animal protein and have decimated the wild animal population. They raise chickens, dogs, ducks, pigs, and carabao and eat them all but only on special occasions. Rice and vegetables are the daily fare. As a result, the Kalinga seem to crave meat and will eat virtually anything from the animal kingdom. When the occasional animal strays into a village area, it is killed and consumed with great enthusiasm.

Apparently, this applies to insects as well. People around the globe have eaten bugs for millennia, of course, and the Kalinga routinely consume at least sixteen different species of insects. I don't recall seeing many insects at all during my stay. Except for the pesky fleas, I saw more insects on my dinner plate than flying or creeping around my house. Guina-ang was too high in elevation for mos-

Ants and ant eggs for breakfast. (James Skibo)

quitoes, and the cockroach, resident in every corner of the globe for hundreds of millions of years, was nonexistent. Given that the village was in a tropical rainforest one might expect a proliferation of insects and endless torment for the human inhabitants, but in this case the climate plus the villagers' propensity to eat anything alive made daily life relatively bug free.

Around breakfast on a morning when I wasn't making pottery observations, Amboy appeared at my door and invited me to his house. His brother had killed a bat. One never refuses invitations for food in the Pasil Valley, a custom that had me eating half a dozen meals on some days, so off I went. Now, however, I was prepared to act less enthusiastically to avoid my ant mistake. The extended family was assembled in Amboy's house and his mother-in-law had cooked some extra rice for the occasion. As coffee was served, Amboy's brother triumphantly recalled how he had found and killed the large fruit bat. I remember little of the story because I was anxious about the entree.

Like all meat, the bat was chopped into small pieces and boiled. The pot was set in the center of the group and everyone helped

Cooking a large pot of rice. (James Skibo, photographer)

himself to a piece of the dark, rich meat. I chose my piece carefully, trying to avoid the feet, head, or any other disturbing portion. Seeing what looked like a little drumstick, I seized it and nibbled with caution. It was rich and gamy, but I too had started to crave meat after months of rice and vegetables, so I licked my bone clean. While I ate I avoided looking at Amboy because he was busy crunching on the bat's head. Happily, the bat morsels went quickly, and my eating strategy allowed others time to finish things off before I had to dig for seconds. When they asked how I liked it, I simply said it was good but not my favorite meat.

Food taboos or forbidden foods exist in every society, but in each case it is purely a cultural creation. While some types of insects or plants are toxic, the grand majority of living things is potential human food. Sitting atop the food chain gives our species a tremendous menu. But what people consider appropriate food varies widely. Americans do not eat dog, horse, guinea pig, or cat; in other parts of the world these species are consumed routinely. We can have such negative reaction to the mere thought of consuming bugs or bats that we assume there must be something genetic about this aversion. Such is the power of culture.

Typical meal of rattan root (l), rice, rattan-root broth, and sweetened coffee. (James Skibo)

Of course, I knew that the Kalinga were a people with few food taboos and anticipated I would be exposed to many exotic dishes. Prior to the start of the project, Bill routinely told stories, usually during lunch, about munching on dog, tail or similar delights, so I figured I was prepared. But I was surprised to find that I even had trouble eating chicken, duck, and pork. Not only was I captive of my food taboos, but I also came face-to-face with strong, culturally held rules governing food preparation and what parts of an animal are edible.

One night I was invited to a house for chicken. I have probably eaten chicken at least once a week for my entire life; this was a food I understood and knew I could enjoy. When I am about to prepare chicken, I see it for the first time under plastic wrap. The killing, plucking, and cleaning are far removed from my life. That night my host brought the live chicken in the house and sat next to me. According to Kalinga practice, he proceeded to slit the chicken's throat and collected the blood in a dish as the bird fought desperately. After a minute or so, it became motionless and the plucking began. Kalinga kitchens are small, usually only about eight to twelve feet square, so feathers filled the room and the smell of fresh blood permeated the air. Big feathers were simply plucked; smaller ones were removed by singeing the carcass in the fire, giving rise to an acrid smell. My host then opened the chicken, removed the internal organs, and added them to the blood in the dish. The raw viscera and blood combination, *paluton*, was our appetizer. Eating some did little to increase my appetite.

My hosts diced the chicken from beak to claw and dumped it in boiling water. Twenty minutes later they served it with the broth. The room was dim, and I reached with hesitation into the pot and came up with a foot. I dropped it back into the pot hoping no one had seen my first catch and fished grimly for a part that I could eat. I finally found something and worked on it carefully, face-to-face with my own culturally determined ideas about what is food and what is not.

Prior to my departure for the Philippines, Carol Kramer, the ethnoarchaeologist mentioned earlier, offered me some advice on food. Her extensive fieldwork in Iran and India caused her to develop some useful responses on encountering unpalatable foods. She would either claim that the food was taboo in her religion, which is a reply that most people of the world will respect, or in India she would claim to be fasting, a culturally accepted means of declining food. Curiosity and hunger had kept me from resorting to a similar strategy, but I was tempted to use it one afternoon. An entire house had been dismantled, carried piece by piece to a new location, and then reassembled. House moving was an occasion for celebration, and we were to feast on dog.

Among the Kalinga, dog is reserved for special occasions, as is the case with other Asian peoples. Dog eating, however, may be one of the strongest American food taboos. For many Americans, dogs are family members and eating Lassie would be tantamount to cannibalism. I had never considered boiling any of my family's series of dogs, assuming I guess that some ancient bond between canines and people was at work. Dogs were probably the first domesticated animals, at about 11,000 B.C. Since then they have been our companions and even "man's best friend." Many prehistoric Native American groups, for example, buried their dogs alongside

A house under construction. (Reprinted by permission of the Arizona State Museum, William Longacre photo)

other loved ones, and Americans today continue something of the tradition in official pet cemeteries. We like to think that our abhorrence of dog as a main course—or even an appetizer—stems from friendship with our loyal friends. Taboos regarding eating horse probably developed for the same reason, although if most Americans were forced to choose they could more easily barbecue a horse steak than a dog burger.

The Kalinga owned dogs but the animals lived on the edge of starvation and scavenged or stole most of their food. They were treated harshly and never befriended. The dogs had short hair, a curled tail, and were small to medium in size. Despite a long history of selection by humans for various characteristics, it is a biological curiosity that when dogs are left alone to breed, as they are in many impoverished cities throughout the world, they don't revert into wolves but into animals that look just like the Kalinga dogs.

I assumed that because the Kalinga treated their dogs more like livestock than friends it would be easier for me to appreciate them in their culinary aspect. The indifferent treatment by the Kalinga toward them made me hope these dogs would be vicious and unloving animals. As a youngster I delivered an afternoon newspaper and was often terrorized by a dog. At the time I had daily fantasies of the animal spinning slowly on my father's backyard rotisserie. So if the Kalinga dogs were treated like livestock and behaved like curs, I thought it would enable me to rise above my culture's food taboos. But the dogs were not vicious. They wanted their ears scratched and were starved for food and human attention. Random breeding had created a generic dog, but even generations of abuse could not change their spirit.

Consequently I felt uneasy when dinner, sensing trouble, was dragged into the house. The dog was brought near the fire, next to me. This time I arose and busied myself counting the pots stored in the rafters as the dog was butchered.

After an hour, the meal was ready and the workers who had moved the house gathered to feast. Chopped-up dog looked like any other Kalinga-prepared meat, so I selected an unrecognizable piece and ate it carefully. I was surprised to see that many dogs had gathered outside and were eagerly awaiting the discarded bones. The canine cannibalism somehow made my taboo-breaking more acceptable. I pushed my way to the pot for another piece. The dark, greasy meat tasted a lot like Kalinga pork.

Having survived this ordeal, I felt that I possessed a new-found power. If I could eat dog, then I thought I must be free of all food taboos. But I soon encountered two foods that were impossible for me to eat.

One warm afternoon as I walked backed to my house after observing and participating in a lunch meal, I noticed the putrid smell of decaying flesh. Growing up in the northern woodlands, where deer outnumber people, had made me familiar with the smell. In the forest the smell of a rotting deer carcass announces itself hundreds of feet before you arrive. It is the kind of odor that makes one want to shower immediately, and if there is something that smells worse on this planet I have not discovered it. I worked on some notes in the first floor of my house, to avoid the heat, but the smell got only stronger. Curious, I walked into the plaza with an upturned nose and asked my assistants, who were returning for some afternoon data collection, about the source of the awful odor. It seemed a carabao had fallen from a cliff and had been discovered only when it started to smell. This was certainly a major loss to some Guina-ang family; an American equivalent would be to have a brand-new uninsured car totaled. Amboy and Joseph went on to explain that the family had dragged the carcass to their house and was in the process of butchering it. The smell progressively worsened as they began the long process of boiling the entire animal. I was nauseated and, during the rest of the afternoon, repeatedly asked all my assistants, "Doesn't that smell bad to you?" Each time, they agreed it did not smell good, and I was overjoyed to learn that Amboy usually refused to eat decaying meat. The anticipated but dreaded dinner invitation soon came.

Dog, bat, or even the intestines of a chicken do not smell or look too bad once cooked. Eating dog, for example, merely required that I think of it as pork. But I knew even before I arrived for dinner that my nose would not allow me any rationalizations. Americans eat rotten meat routinely, I told myself, in that cooking is simply a process that speeds up decay. Such thoughts were of little use as I walked into the house and gazed at the once-festering carabao head now boiling in the largest available metal pot. The smell was simply overpowering. Thankfully, I had done some research in this house a few days earlier and had gotten to know the woman, who was fairly proficient in English. I explained to her that I was honored to be invited but that the smell made me unable to share their dead carabao. She smiled and said it was not a problem, so I had some rice, excused myself early, went to my house and took a bath—that is, poured water over my head.

After a couple of months in Guina-ang and many servings of ants and even one experience with roasted locust, I considered myself a seasoned bug eater. Having a steaming heap of ants and ant eggs placed before me was never one of my greatest joys, but I could eat them with relative indifference. With a little imagination I could even believe I was eating finely chopped lettuce mixed with minced cashew and raisins in a light vinaigrette. For one thing, I was hungry, and at least the bugs were dead.

One Saturday afternoon Amboy suggested that we visit Kaboníyan Falls, located about a half-hour walk from Guina-ang

Cooked carabao head in a large metal pot. (James Skibo)

and named after the founding god in traditional Kalinga religion. It turned out to be a delightful place. When we arrived a group of kids was swimming in a pool below the small falls. Amboy and I quickly disrobed and jumped in. Like most Kalinga, Amboy couldn't seem to pass a stream or river without "taking a bath." A week or so earlier we had been crossing the fast-moving Pasil River and I had followed Amboy's lead into the water. Despite the fact that arsenic from the gold mine upstream had killed all the fish, a cool plunge was hard to resist.

Kaboníyan Falls was even better because we could jump off the rocks and swim under the falls. After an invigorating swim and some horseplay with the local kids, I was drying and relaxing on the warm rocks. Below me the kids and Amboy were reaching under boulders, pulling something off the submerged surface, and then popping it in their mouths. Moving closer I saw they were eating bugs. These water bugs were black and about three-quarters of an inch long. Amboy handed me one and it latched to my finger with surprising strength. I grabbed it by the back and asked how it tasted. "It is sweet," he smiled. He urged me to try it, and I held it closer, its six legs waving and its head moving from side to side. I stared for what seemed like ten minutes, enough time for the bug to tire and wriggle less energetically.

Amboy and the local boys started to poke me and tease me about my obvious reluctance to eat a live bug, but I anticipated feeling this creature fighting back in my mouth or worse yet crawling up my throat after I tried to swallow it. Peer pressure, inevitably, has a way of overcoming reluctance. When I was a kid, similar pressure from my cousin got me to ignore my fear and jump out of a barn's hayloft, maybe ten feet from the ground. But on this day, peer pressure was only partially effective. Surreptitiously I pulled off the bug's legs to ensure it stayed swallowed but causing its head to thrash with renewed desperation. I turned my back and pinched the head. Now, convinced that the bug was sufficiently immobile, I turned to my tormentors and defiantly popped the mutilated treat into my mouth. I crunched down and there was a small explosion of sweet juice that tasted remarkably like a blueberry.

For Americans, few aspects of our lives are more private than the elimination of our own waste. Discussing matters of personal hygiene is generally taboo, as it is in many cultures. Euphemisms are often evidence for a taboo; take for example the many terms in English for the room where waste elimination usually occurs. Even anthropologists, who like to think of themselves as being above taboos, are reluctant to discuss how one "goes to the bathroom." I still do not know of a single anthropological study dedicated to this topic. This fact surprised me at first because I had thought that no aspect of human behavior had gone unexplored by anthropology. We discuss male and female circumcision, penis piercing, and all matters of sex in exacting detail, but no one has explored, cross-culturally, an act that everyone in the world performs daily. Interested people can find out certain bathroom rituals by traveling to different areas of the world or by perusing ethnographies in which anthropologists discuss local toilet customs, but a general treatise remains to be written. We know that there is great variation worldwide. For example, many people of the Middle East wash themselves by pouring water and scrubbing with the left hand, which is then never used for eating; and the French have sanitized the process with Monsieur Bidet's invention for washing the external genitals and posterior parts of the body. Americans seem to prefer toilet paper, which is wasteful and certainly less effective than any of the washing methods.

I was not always fascinated by human defecation, perfectly content with the taboo on discussion, but that all changed as I was about to embark on this project. Knowing that people without running water, electricity, or roads would lack elegant facilities, I demanded some specifics from Bill Longacre. He told me that the Kalinga answer their needs near the edge of the village and clean themselves with smooth stones or grass. Bill knew the specifics of the process, having already spent a year in Dangtalan, but he held the best part for the end. He advised that it would be best to have a stick to keep the pigs away.

The pigs are Kalinga chamber maids and get quite excited at the prospect of a warm meal. I winced at the thought of fending off charging pigs while otherwise engaged, and concluding that the Kalinga don't get a chance to scan *People* magazine during the process. After I had been in Guina-ang for a time I grew accustomed to the local waste-reclamation process. Children often played in the plaza near my house, toddlers running about without pants. The squeal of a pig usually signaled that a youngster was answering nature's call. A nearby pig or two would wait impatiently for the child to finish and then move in quickly. One day a child was apparently taking too long, for I saw an anxious porker butt the kid out of the way.

Despite an occasional run-in of my own with an eager pig, I considered the Kalinga method of dealing with children's toilet practices civilized. As soon as children could walk they learned to relieve themselves outside with none of the turmoil that often surrounds the "potty training" of young America. Hundreds of books for parents are devoted to this topic and many latter-life psychological problems are traced to unpleasant experiences associated with learning the American custom. Kalinga children who do not yet walk simply go without pants or undergarments and relieve themselves whenever and wherever they desire. Babies are usually wrapped in a cloth when parents or friends hold them, which is the closest thing to our custom of diapers. As the Kalinga children crawl around they simply "go" on the bamboo floor and the mess is quickly cleaned up or rinsed away. A baby caught in the act would be held out an open window, with much apparent delight. We put diapers on our children and sometimes make them sit for extended periods in their waste. This inhumane system is a relatively recent phenomenon, as my parents grew up with a Kalinga-like system. It is unfortunate that we ever got away from such a method, which perhaps became necessary with the advent of wall-to-wall carpeting.

Thankfully, Bill Longacre said that the first order of business after arriving in Guina-ang would be to construct a bathroom. When I arrived in Dangtalan I was indeed impressed by Bill's set-up; he had paid Kalinga men to build a bathroom, complete with a porcelain toilet, plus a washroom with running water supplied by an overhead tank. This was luxury. Our Guina-ang set-up was not as elegant. Upon our arrival, Kalinga men constructed a woven-bamboo hut with two rooms. One room was for bathing and the other was the comfort room and housed the more standard Asian squat toilet.

One of the first toilets with seats was used by Egyptian royalty about 1350 B.C. Europeans continued the toilet seat tradition, possibly to emulate the royals. Apparently there was also a functional reason for the use of toilet seats by European royalty, since they were often too obese to defecate in any other way. One wonders if publishers may have been involved in the seated system because of the well-known, though infrequently discussed, fact that a good deal of reading takes place while on the throne. But all over Asia the squat system is the norm, and having used it I would have to say that recreational reading is not possible. Not only does one fatigue quickly (*People* articles would have to be even shorter), but the participant must concentrate on balance, for the cost of inattention is too great.

Our system in Guina-ang worked very well. The squat toilet was simply a hole in a concrete slab, flushed by a bucket of water. The waste collected in an underground drain field below the comfort room. I found this system acceptable as long as I had an ample supply of toilet paper. I believe I can withstand various forms of mental and physical abuse and exist without many of the amenities now considered basic to American life, but without toilet paper I have a hard time functioning. Consequently I tried to make sure I had always an adequate supply and I also stashed numerous rolls, like an alcoholic hiding bottles, in the event of a shortage. Several times it was necessary to break into the secret stash because supply trips to Tabuk were infrequent. In such instances I hesitantly prioritized the paper items in my possession, novels at one end and my notebooks at the other, that could serve as T.P. in an emergency.

Personal hygiene is also determined by one's culture. Americans, as a whole, are obsessed with personal cleanliness, but this was not always the case. During the sixteenth and seventeenth centuries Europeans and Americans lived in what we would now consider an unsanitary state. Bathing was extremely infrequent and human waste, in many cases, was simply thrown into the street. By today's standards an average citizen from the period would be considered unclean. Even well into the twentieth century, prior to the widespread adoption of indoor plumbing and hot tap water, a bath was still a luxury. Bathing was commonly a once-per-week undertaking because of the inconvenience of carrying and heating water, and the same water often served more than one bather.

It is common for Americans today, however, to bathe or shower daily. Certainly there are many jobs, including mining, roofing, brick laying, and excavating an archaeological site, that involve a lot of dirt and grime, but most Americans have jobs in which they do not become soiled. I shower every day despite the fact that a hard day of writing and teaching does not leave me dirty. Clearly, Americans' notions of personal cleanliness have gone beyond what is necessary to maintain good health and into another realm entirely.

The Roman period offers a parallel. Bathing for the Roman citizen was considered a social duty, and public baths were found throughout the empire, some capable of holding as many as 1,600 people. The Romans too were daily bathers; certain emperors bathed half-a-dozen or more times per day. The typical routine for the upper levels of Roman society was to begin bathing in the early afternoon and proceed through a luxurious ritual that could include steam rooms, scrubbing, oils and ointments, and warm and cold baths.

In the case of turn-of-the-millennium Americans, it might be argued that they have elevated body rituals to the point of religion. Anthropologist Horace Miner, in fact, did just that in his examination of the American bathroom, which he refers to as a holy shrine. Although Miner's article is written tongue-in-cheek, it is still revealing. Pretending to be an outsider and learning about American (which he calls "Nacirema") culture, Miner examines body rituals that take place in one or more holy shrines in every Nacirema house. For example, Miner makes the point that these rituals are private and secret and that much time is spent in front of the charm box (medicine cabinet) located above the holy font (sink). The charm box is filled with potions that are obtained from medicine men and then never discarded because of their magical powers. At the holy font each person performs daily rituals that involve splashing the face with water followed by the mouth-rite (brushing teeth). Failure to do so, according to Miner, jeopardizes social standing and may require a happy holy-mouth-man (dentist). His point is that rules regarding personal cleanliness are also culturally defined.

Being an observer yet a captive of my own culture, I was pleased to learn that the Kalinga also like to bathe daily. Many of the early travelers also reported that the Kalinga were "clean." Nor did the Kalinga consider it strange that we wanted a separate, private area for bathing. Like a Roman, I usually bathed in the early afternoon during a break between the lunch and dinner data collection. The village of Guina-ang got its water from a spring in the mountains. Bamboo and metal pipes carried water to half-a-dozen locations throughout the village where the locals bathed. They also washed clothes and dishes, and collected the household water supply there. Women often bathed after washing clothes during the day, but many men waited until dark for a bit more privacy. By supplying money for pipe, we were given the luxury of water delivered right to our bath, which kept the plastic tub full. The bathing process simply involved dumping cold water over my head, but I enjoyed it tremendously and looked forward to it as one of my luxuries, especially since temperatures in a smoky kitchen could sometimes exceed 100 degrees F.

I was constantly reminded of the many similarities between Guina-ang and daily life in a small American town. In either place, for example, the gossip network would insure that anyone's business was everyone's business. There is an adaptive element to this in that it can act as a form of social control and as a check on deviant behavior, but village gossip can also make it difficult for a person to reform or change. Asked about another villager, a Kalinga might speak of events that happened thirty years ago. You cannot escape your past in a small town. But one difference between most American towns and Guina-ang was that in the latter the lack of privacy extended into one's own home. In the United States we think of our homes as private refuges. We can feel relatively free there to do what we please without fear of opprobrium from our neighbors (unless the curtains are open). In Guina-ang the thin bamboo walls and the tightly packed houses meant that even behavior within a private residence was subject to public scrutiny.

I suspect I was known as a man who hated chickens. In fact I did develop a hatred of chickens, which are permitted to roam inside houses with only an occasional protest. The problem was that the chickens were covered with fleas, as were the other animals, and my feet and ankles were always peppered with red flea bites. I got many more bites in homes that allowed complete freedom for chickens. In my house, aside from the fleas, the chickens were constantly eating our stored food. For example, someone would give us a bunch of bananas as a gift; if they were left unprotected, the chickens quickly ate them.

It was common for chickens to hop into our kitchen during dinner and try to steal some food. Shooing them away was just a temporary fix because they returned within minutes, so I turned to slightly more forceful means. I started throwing things. One evening during dinner at my house I picked up a spoon and beaned an intruder in the back of the head. It squawked loudly, quickly fluttered out, and did not return. It became a nightly ritual. When a spoon was not within reach I would throw a shoe or anything handy. It got to the point where a raised hand was sufficient to send the chickens scampering. To my joy, this even worked in other houses. When no one was looking I could raise my hand and immediately banish the flea-infested little thieves.

One of the many gravity fed "water spots" in Guina-ang used for washing clothes and dishes, taking baths, and household water. (James Skibo)

One evening after I had successfully dispersed a small flock of chickens, Pascuala, my neighbor and landlady, said through the wall, "Mr. James, you don't like chickens." She was right, but not wanting to seem too eccentric, I explained that I merely resented them eating my food. Mysteriously, the windows in the kitchen, where most of the chickens entered, were fitted with bamboo shutters. I might as well have been winging the chickens in the plaza before the entire town because they knew exactly what was going on in the "privacy" of my own house. People in Guina-ang are probably still saying, "Mr. James was a nice guy, but he was pretty strange with the chickens."

Tightly packed houses and thin bamboo walls did have some advantages. With slightly raised voices many people could actually carry on a conversation or at least exchange information with neighbors. A number of mornings, as I began my research day in a household before sunrise, I would hear a neighbor requesting a light for their fire. Women anxious about my visit often had their fires going already, and their children were sent out, after one of the through-the-wall requests, with a burning stick for a neighbor in order to conserve matches. I was uncomfortable with this between-the-wall system because it always felt like such an intrusion, but Pascuala talked to us so frequently that it soon seemed normal. I eventually incorporated it into my morning wake-up ritual. I was always up by 5:00 A.M. to start my predawn research, and Pascuala was awake as well lighting her morning fire and heating coffee. I started each of these days by simply saying, "Good morning, Pascuala," and she would answer, always with a slight giggle, "Good morning, Mr. James."

Every Sunday morning the bell on the chapel rang, continuing periodically until enough people had gathered for a prayer service. Inevitably, the ringing bell prompted Pascuala to say, "Ahhh, Sunday." The Kalinga, like most non-Western peoples, did not share our concept of time. Days, weeks, months, and years are concepts that have been imposed upon them. The passage of time for the Kalinga was measured by the beginning and end of the wet and dry seasons, the ripening of rice, and the reproductive cycles of animals. But someone in our village had a calendar and was responsible for ringing the bell every Sunday morning.

Religion for the Kalinga was a complex mix of traditional Kalinga beliefs and the various Christian approaches introduced by missionaries since the beginning of the Spanish Period. Catholicism, a number of Protestant sects, and now even a Baptist group had moved deep into the Kalinga homeland by the late 1980s. In Guina-ang, there was a church built by the Saint Paul Society and the Belgian priests, and there had been a strong Catholic influence since early in the twentieth century. The priest occasionally made it to Guina-ang for Sunday Mass (once during my stay), but usually a prayer service was conducted by the residents. The persistent tolling of the bell piqued my curiosity and one Sunday I decided to walk down to the chapel. I was raised a Catholic, so this was one part of Kalinga life that I felt would not be unfamiliar.

The small green church was soundly built of sawn lumber and was easily the biggest building in Guina-ang. I walked into the church, which had rough benches for pews and a wooden altar and lectern, and quietly took a seat among ten or so other churchgoers.

As the bell rang again I asked when the service started and was told "by and by." Eventually the congregation grew to twenty people and things got under way. It started with a roof-raising hymn, which I joined with enthusiasm. Most of the worshipers were women, and I was impressed by their singing ability. Several men, however, led the prayer service, which included readings from the Bible, commentary by the leader, and then a general discussion of scripture.

Despite the fact that the chapel was quite full, it represented less than 5 percent of the 500 Guina-ang residents. When asked, most of the villagers would say they were Christian, but the poor attendance at the prayer service suggested that they, like many Americans, were not active in their faith. The presence of the Belgian priest one Sunday increased attendance to capacity, but this could still be considered a poor showing. The likely reason is that the Kalinga, though they seemed to welcome Christianity, still maintained strong ties to their traditional faith. Like many non-Western peoples that have been approached by missionaries of every stripe, the Kalinga religious beliefs have become an amalgam of the new and the old.

Traditional Kalinga religion has a creator deity, Kabuníyan, who is the supreme being but rather ambivalent about the world. The core of Kalinga religion and ritual focuses on spirits, or *anitos*. As in many societies, the Kalinga consider the spirit world and the earthly world at odds. The supernatural world is filled with spirits, which may be deceased relatives, that are responsible for such misfortunes as sickness, crop failure, or even death. A person who has experienced a run of bad luck has done something to anger the spirits. Therefore, the core of the Kalinga religion focused on appeasing the responsible elements in the supernatural. A shaman was called upon to serve as a medium, identify the responsible spirit, and prescribe a remedy. Kalinga often referred to the local mediums, who were always women, as "quack doctors," but during my stay quack doctors were still called into service. The typical ritual performed by the medium involved sacrificing an animal, often a chicken, and then offering prayers to identify and placate the spirits.

I was not the first visitor to the Mountain Province to have noted the lack of privacy afforded by the single-room, bamboo-walled houses. Many travelers have specifically mentioned that the sounds of love-making could be heard during the night. The prudishness of the nineteenth and early twentieth centuries no doubt made these descriptions by Westerners especially titillating. Of course, such articles or reports also had the requisite photographs of bare-breasted young women, which somehow escaped the censor's gaze. As an avid reader of the *National Geographic* during my youth, I appreciated the naked-lady section, but the irony is striking. Although most American families would not have permitted pornography in their households, photos of naked black or brown women on the coffee table were a different matter. Descriptions of non-Western people, during that era, provided one of the only means for mainstream America to talk openly about sex. Regarding the Kalinga, I expected now that the older descriptions were somewhat exaggerated, because I never heard any sounds of passion through the thin walls whatsoever. Sometimes exhaustion or gin made me a sound sleeper; more often I was awake during the long nights, which afforded plenty of opportunity to listen for the night noises of Guina-ang.

In fact it was deathly quiet, the only sounds being an occasional barking dog or a squealing pig rooted by someone seeking midnight relief. The thought of tripping over a pig, which had tusks and was capable of an angry fit, usually kept me confined to my room at night. When nature called, I just stood at the edge of my porch or used my window. I enjoyed these porch trips because it was good to feel the silence and to be completely alone after a day filled with constant noise and stares. Sometimes I would stand for a half hour or more, enjoying the peace and stargazing if the sky was clear. On moonless periods particularly, the stars were intensely bright. A nighttime sky unspoiled by light pollution and smog is an unforgettable sight.

But I admit that during these quiet periods my thoughts often turned to sex. I did not hear the sounds of sex, and I wondered how adults managed relations in a small room packed with five or ten people. Some Kalinga houses had two rooms, which offered some privacy; many had only one. A typical household included the parents, often with an infant sleeping in the arms of its mother, and several other children, all within ten feet or less. The frequency of births in young families proved this arrangement was no deterrent to parental conjugation, however. And the arrangement that baffled me most was that of the houses with several couples and up to four generations under the same roof—Amboy's place for instance. At the time of the study, he lived in a house with his wife and infant child, his in-laws, and his wife's grandmother.

In my culture we demand complete privacy for romance. We go to such lengths for privacy and are so successful at it that many American children have grown up convinced that their parents never have sex. The architecture of our houses reflects this emphasis, and those parental how-to books also have a chapter that provides guidance to the parents who are having trouble maintaining a sex life after the arrival of kids. Not only will these books give some helpful hints, such as putting a movie in the VCR or taking advantage of back-to-back Barney and Sesame Street episodes on Sunday, but they also provide step-by-step guidance if children "catch parents." Kalinga parents would see this as absolutely nutty.

Margaret Mead, in her classic Pacific-island study of the Samoans, thought that some of the problems of adolescence in America could be attributed to our avoidance of sexuality. Samoans, Mead found, had a more open attitude toward sex and also fewer problems with their adolescents. Mead argued that these behaviors were related and that Americans would have less adolescent rebellion if the barriers to discussion of sex were removed. Outwardly at least, America is seemingly more open to sexuality today than it was during Mead's time, yet it is still mostly a taboo subject in our homes. I would be uncomfortable with adopting Kalinga sleeping arrangements, but there seems to be some real wisdom in the openness of Kalinga ways.

As a baby-boomer I take for granted many things that my parents did not have, like television, indoor plumbing, and even electricity. My father talks about walking home after dark from a friend's house on a neighboring farm a mile or so away. Without the aid of lights he could still find his way back through the fields and patches of forest because he had taken this trip so many times. Tripping over a sleeping cow was the only real danger. I thought of this story during the occasions when I had to walk home after staying at someone's house past dark. On moonlit nights this was less of a problem because there was usually enough light for me to negotiate the winding paths. Guina-ang was built on a hill that has been terraced, like the Kalinga rice fields, with a number of eight-foot-high stone walls that had to be climbed or descended to move about the village. The steps going up and down the walls were formed naturally by rocks falling into place over the years. Nobody had actually gone to the effort of building stairs. During the day it was not a problem, but at night these obstacles could be dangerous. Sometimes I remembered to bring a flashlight, which I would click on at the walls or for general reference. The Kalinga negotiated the obstacles quickly and effortlessly, night or day. Sometimes my assistants had to walk me home, amused at my inability to negotiate the terrain by night without tripping or using my flashlight.

Robert Lawless, a cultural anthropologist who did some research in the Pasil Valley in the early 1970s, speaks of a similar experience. In his first weeks among the Kalinga, he had trouble keeping up with the locals on the slippery, steep mountain trails; he recalls lagging twenty minutes behind two men carrying a woman on a stretcher. Eventually he become more adept at walking on the treacherous trails, and by the end of his stay he could even walk some of the common trails at night unaided by light.

Settling into the rhythm of village life and the daily regime of data collection, I began to forget the outside world. During my first month I was desperate for news, especially since so many interesting things seemed to be happening in my world back in Tucson. The country was in the middle of the 1988 presidential campaign, the citizens of Arizona were poised to impeach their governor, Evan Mecham, and the Arizona Wildcat basketball team was in the NCAA tournament (eventually making it to the Final Four). In Manila I followed these and other issues in the papers with the distant accompaniment of automatic weapons, the latest coup attempt on Corazon Aquino. After I arrived in the Pasil Valley, however, these issues faded as I became increasingly immersed in the daily lives of Guina-ang people. Now the important news for me became who was sick, who was getting married, the productivity of the rice harvest, broken water pipes, and how a family was going to pay for their youngest child's college tuition. Their world had quickly become my world, and presidential campaigns and even the latest news about the Philippine coup seemed distant and unimportant. This all changed one afternoon as an armed unit of the Cordillera Peoples Liberation Army (CPLA) made its way to Guina-ang. In an instant I was wrenched from the life of an isolated villager into the bigger picture of national politics and armed conflict.

I was in our house working on my journal and research forms when I heard excited and tense voices outside. Going out I was told that an armed unit of the CPLA was just beyond the village. "What should I do?" I asked my assistant, Edita, who was approaching my house.

"I don't know."

"Do I have anything to worry about?" I persisted. "I could run or hide if you think I am in danger."

"I don't think you need to do that," she offered. As I stood there pondering, everyone disappeared except a few curious children. It became clear that the villagers were not afraid for their safety but they were unsure about mine. They did not know my politics or who I was aligned with, and their nervous discussion outside was an attempt to determine my degree of danger. Apparently they obviously concluded that they did not know but gave me ample warning to flee if I felt threatened.

I wondered if I should be afraid of these armed men. The CPLA was composed of former NPA members. Corazon Aquino's first act as president was to halt Marcos's Chico Dam Project, which prompted many Kalinga and other Mountain Province people to put down their weapons. With government support, the CPLA was formed and recruited some of these soldiers to now fight the remaining units of the NPA. Superficially, this would have seemed to pose no danger for me, but politics in the Philippines is never so simple.

Our research group considered itself apolitical, but we still had to align ourselves with certain groups in order to work in the Philippines. Technically, our research effort was jointly sponsored by the University of Arizona and the University of the Philippines.

The latter had a reputation as a hotbed of political insurrection and for having close ties with the NPA. The people in the village knew of this association, which probably accounted for their uncertainty about my safety in the presence of the CPLA. But I was not overtly allied with the NPA, or any political position, and I hoped this could be made clear despite my affiliation with the University of the Philippines. It would have been easy to hide, but I decided to sit tight.

I was lying on my bed reading when I looked up to see a young man about my age sitting on the porch bench outside my door with an AK–47 automatic rifle resting across his knees. I stood up and said hello, noticing that while he was not Kalinga he doubtless was a member of the Mountain Province groups. His hair was much longer than was the local custom, and he wore green army fatigues and a faded T-shirt. He also said hello and glanced up at me but then turned away so that I could not see his face. I decided against offering to shake his hand.

In excellent English, he asked me what I was doing in Guina-ang. I described our project and added how we were helping the people by doing things like providing medicine and fixing water pipes. I summed up the project quickly, assuming that he had already learned as much. He then asked if we were affiliated with the University of the Philippines. I hesitated and he glanced at me again. Oh shit, I thought. He probably knew that answer too, so I decided against deception. I told him that it was necessary for Americans to be affiliated with a Philippine university, but we were anthropologists interested only in the Kalinga culture and their pottery. I also mentioned Bill Longacre's name several times, deciding that I was not going to face a firing squad alone. The CPLA man seemed satisfied with my answer. Ten minutes later he said good-bye softly and walked off.

After a moment I stepped onto my porch and between the houses could see his group sitting under the shade of large tree. They were relaxing, smoking cigarettes, and talking quietly. The only villagers visible were the ubiquitous children, no doubt collecting intelligence for their parents. Confident that the episode was over, I went back into my house. It suddenly seemed that danger was close to the surface in Guina-ang, despite appearances.

CHAPTER 5

The Bamboo Classroom

AS DIRECTOR OF OUR PROJECT, Bill Longacre spent most of his days dealing with the logistics of keeping the research going smoothly in the three villages, Dangtalan, Dalupa, and Guina-ang. In addition to his own research agenda, Bill was the captain of our forever-sinking ship and wore many hats: business manager, banker, counselor, and teacher. The project, for a time the largest employer in the Pasil River Valley, had more than twenty local people on the payroll at various points. This required lots of cash and frequent trips to the nearest bank, an arduous and sometimes dangerous journey. Getting the wad of money for the monthly payroll past the holduppers was a constant challenge. Moreover, there was a steady stream of supplies moving into the Pasil Valley—tempting to the Kalinga men who had turned to the dark side.

On one trip back from Tabuk, riding a truck loaded with food and necessities, Bill and a group of Kalinga assistants startled three armed men near the head of the foot trail to Dangtalan. Jeepney transport to and from Tabuk occurred daily but rarely at a predictable time. The holduppers had dozed off in the warm afternoon sun waiting for easy pickings. They jumped up when the jeepney passed, but the driver gunned the engine and quickly rounded the corner. Unfortunately, the trailhead was less than a quarter of a mile farther, and, while the supplies were being unloaded, the holduppers covered the distance on foot. They started shooting as soon as they rounded the last corner, but the extra minutes had given the jeepney driver time to roar off and for Bill's assistants to seek cover. Most of the Kalinga men bounded down the steep trail toward Dangtalan, but in order to negotiate the slippery trail Bill needed first to put in his contact lenses, which he could not wear during the dusty trip from Tabuk. So, bullets whizzing past his head, Bill carefully applied his contacts before initiating a hasty descent.

But the true act of courage, enough to make even Indiana Jones envious, was performed by Roberto, Bill's primary assistant. As the holduppers approached, guns blazing, Roberto sat down defiantly on the pile of hastily unloaded supplies. Roberto was an important Kalinga man, and the sight of him perched atop the supplies seemed enough to deter the bandits. He was banking on Kalinga deterrence, not unlike the Cold War American and Soviet version. It was a calculated risk, but Roberto relied on a certainty that his death at the hands of the holduppers would prompt his relatives and other Dangtalan residents to seek a bloody revenge.

Stresses of running the project went beyond holduppers. Bill was responsible for hiring, and sometimes firing, the assistants and keeping the Arizona and Filipino students safe and at least somewhat happy. He had to teach us how to live and work in this remote setting and also occasionally served as referee among budding scholars trying to find their research niches. Small differences of personality between students or personnel could become exaggerated from living and working together for long periods in close quarters.

Confronted with these and many other crises on a daily basis in Dangtalan, Bill occasionally made an escape to Guina-ang. Not exactly a resort spa, Guina-ang was still far enough removed from the project's Dangtalan headquarters to provide an occasional bit of breathing room. Unannounced, Bill would come trudging into Guina-ang carrying a bottle of Collectors, the closest thing to sipping whiskey available in the Mountain Province. Compared to the soda-bottle gin that I had become accustomed to drinking, this was like Chivas Regal.

At dusk, when the clamor of village activity began to subside, we would sit down in my small bamboo house and start on the Collectors. I would light the oil lamp and we would begin discussing fieldwork problems and concerns. It was an opportunity to tell Bill how the research was progressing, and we shared Dangtalan

Bill Longacre watching a woman make pots. (James Skibo)

and Guina-ang gossip or news from home. Our discussions shifted from the presidential race in the States to problems with employees. As the night wore on and the Collectors slowly drained, our talk usually turned to archaeology and archaeological history. I have taken more archaeology courses in my university days than I can remember and have read countless books on the subject, yet I learned a lot more about archaeological history during these few sessions in the bamboo classroom.

Our discussions focused on the people—the archaeologists— much more than on what was discovered or what theories were proposed. Because archaeology is such a new science, oral history is still possible. Thomas Jefferson is often given credit for the first scientific excavation in the United States when he (his slaves) trenched a burial mound on his Virginia plantation, but American archaeology really did not become scientific in any meaningful sense until the twentieth century. Archaeologists in Bill's generation, who began careers in midcentury, witnessed an amazing growth and development.

To get a perspective on the rapid development of North American archaeology, consider three generations of faculty at the University of Arizona: Emil Haury, Bill Longacre, and Mike Schiffer. Byron Cummings founded the Department of Archaeology in 1915, but Haury became the head in 1937 and changed it to the Department of Anthropology. Haury was trained at Harvard and among his many accomplishments he defined two of the major prehistoric culture groups in the Southwestern United States. In the early part of the twentieth century, it was possible for a man like Haury to be on personal terms with every professional archaeologist in the United States and many foreign archaeologists as well. The initial meetings of the Society for American Archaeology in the mid-1930s consisted of a couple dozen archaeologists—now these meetings have thousands of participants.

In the bamboo classroom, Bill explained to me that by the time he began his career in archaeology he knew *of* each archaeologist. He may not have known each one personally, but he knew where each had trained, research interests, and current employment. When Mike Schiffer and the first wave of baby boomers entered graduate school, college education was no longer restricted to the elite. Yet, while archaeology began to lose its country-club feeling in the1960s and early 1970s, Schiffer was still forced during his initial training (directed, in part, by Bill, who was a young faculty member during Schiffer's graduate years at Arizona) to read something by virtually every important North American archaeologist. Now, at the start of the new millennium, a vast number of people call archaeology their profession. It is difficult even to keep up with a narrow specialty.

Longacre personally witnessed the three main periods in twentieth-century North American archaeology—culture history, New Archaeology, and today's multifaceted approach—but got his first taste of field archaeology near the Caterpillar manufacturing plant, just east of Peoria, Illinois, about thirty miles from where I am writing this page. On free weekends, when not performing as a snare drummer in the Fighting Illini marching band, he helped excavate a site that was in the path of expansion at the Caterpillar plant. The excavation was under the direction of Elaine Bluhm Herold and John McGregor, the latter a professor at the University of Illinois and a major figure in the culture-history period in American archaeology. *Southwestern Archaeology*, McGregor's important book published in 1941, illustrated the interests of this period: placing prehistoric cultures into spatial and temporal categories. The focus then was on description rather than on social or cultural explanation.

The culture-history period began with a heightened interest in the antiquities of the New World during the expansion of Euroamerican settlement into the "West," at the time meaning Ohio, Indiana, and the Midwest. Settlers encountered ruins of great cities, temple pyramids, and exquisite works of art. The most impressive of these ruins, Cahokia, is on the Illinois side of the Mississippi River just east of St. Louis, Missouri. The prehistoric city, part of a much larger Midwest occupation known as the Mississippian, once had as many as 20,000 people, making it one of the largest cities in the *world* at A.D. 1150. At the time, it had a greater population than London. Under the watchful eye of powerful priest-kings, the people of Cahokia built a great enclave covering over five square miles and eventually including more than a hundred burial and temple mounds. It boasted a structure similar to Stonehenge in

Reconstruction of Cahokia at A.D. 1100. Monk's Mound with a temple on the apex and other public facilities and mounds are surrounded by a stockade wall. Note the solar calendar, "wood henge," far left, and some of the thousands of individual houses. (Painting by William R. Iseminger, reproduced by permission of the Cahokia Mounds Museum Society)

Britain but made of great wooden posts. The largest of the mounds, Monks Mound, still stands. It is ten stories high, fourteen acres at its base, and constructed of twenty-two million cubic feet of earth. Plunk down Monks Mound among the pyramids of Giza and it would not be out of place. Few Americans know of this remarkable site, and fewer still have actually climbed to its top to marvel at its size or ponder the significance of this once-great city. There is an irony here because in the days when George Washington was a land speculator in what is now Ohio, it is safe to say that nearly all Americans knew of Cahokia and other impressive ruins encountered during the western expansion. Why the change in attitude?

During the eighteenth and nineteenth centuries Americans had to consider who once lived in grand cities such as Cahokia and built the hundreds of mounds they kept finding up and down the Mississippi drainage. We now know that prehistoric Native Americans were responsible, but for most Euroamericans of the period the notion was preposterous. Many presumed that Native Americans were not only incapable of such accomplishments but that they might have actually conquered and destroyed some great, possibly European, race. There was rampant speculation about the vanished Mound Builders. Hindus, Welshmen, Danes, Vikings, and lost biblical tribes were all suggested. The Mound Builder controversy was even debated in Congress when it appropriated $5,000 for John Wesley Powell, director of the Bureau of Ethnology, to create the Division of Mound Exploration. Powell, a Civil War hero, one-time Illinois State University professor, and first to explore the treacherous rapids of the Grand Canyon, picked Cyrus Thomas in 1882 to head the operation and finally solve the riddle.

Thomas oversaw a remarkably thorough investigation of the mounds. His work is often viewed as the beginning of modern American archaeology. Although he spent most of his time in Washington, his team of researchers scattered over the Midwest investigating hundreds of mounds. This turned out to be the best $5,000 Congress ever spent because Thomas put together an exemplary report of his researchers' findings, proving beyond a doubt that it was the Native Americans alone who were responsible for the impressive ruins.

Why had Native Americans been so quickly dismissed as the Mound Builders? First, European-introduced diseases eliminated up to half the Native American population east of the Mississippi long before any significant European settlement. The Native American groups that Thomas Jefferson saw had undergone tremendous and devastating change in the previous 300 years.

Second, most of the mounds that the Euroamericans first saw as they crossed the Allegheny Mountains in the 1800s were constructed by peoples we now refer to as the Adena and Hopewell. These groups had ceased mound building 300 years prior to Columbus. Even the great city of Cahokia was abandoned in the mid-thirteenth century, long before French voyageurs first explored the Mississippi. By the time Euroamericans arrived, the seat of power had shifted south. Hernando de Soto was searching for gold in North America during the 1500s, but what he found instead were powerful chiefdoms like Coosa, near present-day Carters, Georgia. Vestiges of the old civilization lingered. As late as the 1700s, French traders lived among the last of these chiefdoms.

A final reason Native Americans were so readily dismissed as Mound Builders was simply because it was an attitude that allowed the Euroamericans to keep the moral high ground, at least in their own eyes. It was easier to conquer Native Americans believing them godless savages rather than creators of grand cities and works of art.

Cyrus Thomas led the way to a more scientific archaeology, and there was a flurry of activity as researchers began to investigate the prehistory of the continent on a sounder basis. During this period our Yooper friend Alfred Kidder and other archaeological pioneers fanned into every region seeking to be the first to delineate the prehistoric epochs and inhabitants. I suspect that many contemporary archaeologists envy this original group. Some members of that first wave were highly skilled and others were merely average, but their names are repeated in archaeological courses and their writings consulted by those who still work in the same regions.

Our discussions in the bamboo classroom often turned to the New Archaeology. Bill Longacre got involved in archaeology right at the end of the culture-history period and was instrumental in the development of the New Archaeology. As a graduate student at the University of Chicago, he spent his summers at Paul Martin's field program in Vernon, Arizona. Martin had been an important figure in Southwestern archaeology since the 1920s. His excavation reports from western New Mexico are now considered classics. But his field projects at Vernon and his unique teaching style also had a lasting effect. Every summer Martin would appoint a senior graduate student to lead the summer's excavations. He allowed these leaders relatively free rein to design the excavation and analyze the material, which usually served as a basis for their dissertations. In most field projects the director typically controls what is studied, what questions are asked, and what explanations are rendered. The danger in Martin's style is that one can do some really bad archaeology, as students may not be fully prepared for field responsibility. The upside is that it fosters an environment of creativity and innovation.

At about the same time that Bill Longacre's turn came to lead the excavation and analysis of the pueblo, Carter Ranch, Lewis Binford appeared at the University of Chicago with revolution on his mind. Binford was critical of culture-history archaeology, criticizing it as merely descriptive and devoid of explanation. He argued with passion that archaeology could potentially investigate any topic studied by cultural anthropologists, convincing Longacre and others to refocus their efforts and demonstrate that archaeology and anthropology were one and the same. Longacre's dissertation did not center on pottery descriptions and illustrations of pueblo room types, but on prehistoric social organization and marital residence patterns. Based on the distributions of pottery designs alone, Longacre posited that the twelfth-century pueblo practiced matrilocal residence—newlyweds lived with the wife's family after marriage.

These were tumultuous times in virtually all aspects of American society. In archaeology a group of young scholars (many of them now from the middle class) was tossing aside the approaches of their fathers' generation in favor of ideas that were as different as their appearance. When they weren't experimenting with drugs or discussing ways to avoid the draft, they were forging a new archaeology.

One of the best early examples of the New Archaeology took shape on the banks of the Illinois River, just behind the house of Theodore and Mary Koster. Two young Northwestern University professors, Stuart Streuver and James Brown, put the new approaches to work in one of the most significant excavations in North America. The excavations began in 1969 with only a few test pits, but by the time the site was closed the Kosters' backyard had a hole thirty feet deep. Aside from being a remarkable feat of logistics and engineering, the immense excavation was significant because its researchers were able to document prehistoric life from about 7500 B.C. to A.D. 1200 in a detail never before achieved. Fortuitously, Koster sat on the Illinois River floodplain. Over thousands of years, flood waters periodically covered the prehistoric houses and village features, leaving sediments in their wake and creating an archaeologist's dream: a deeply stratified site. Koster's stratigraphy consisted of at least twelve separate occupational surfaces separated by flood depositions. A seasonal camp with evidence of just a few temporary dwellings at about 6500 B.C. was more than three stories below the present-day corn fields.

What made the Koster excavation and analysis especially unique was its emphasis on reconstructing the climate, diet, and demography

Excavations at the Koster site where archaeologists uncovered fourteen occupation levels extending over 8,700 years. (William R. Iseminger)

of the prehistoric peoples who had lived there and how this changed over millennia of occupation. To do this, the archaeologists did not rely solely on traditional analyses of chert tools or pottery—they devised techniques to recover and analyze plant and animal remains. One clever method was flotation analysis, a technique that permits recovery of small bits of organic matter—often fragments of what people were eating. In flotation analysis a worker dumps sediment from a feature such as a hearth or house floor into water. Tiny fragments of organic matter that can evade even the most skilled excavator, seed remnants and nut shells for instance, float to the surface to be skimmed and dried. To the untrained eye this looks like pond scum, but it contains important clues to what people were eating. Using microscopic analysis, investigators were able to determine that the diet of the Koster people included hickory nuts, deer, turtle, fish, and waterfowl, to name just a few of the identified plant and animal species. Moreover, the investigators looked at animals that are sensitive to subtle environmental changes to provide a remarkable reconstruction of climatic change during Koster's long occupancy.

The Koster excavation energized the picture of hunter-gatherer life on the banks of the Illinois River. This early period, referred to as the Archaic, was similar in many ways to the Mesolithic (or middle stone age) in Europe. Generally speaking, it was a period of more complex hunting and gathering activity situated between the time of the Ice Age mastodon hunters and the agriculturalists and Mound Builders. To put this period in greater perspective, a brief look at the peopling of the New World will be helpful.

At this writing, the general consensus is that the North and South American continents were initially populated sometime after 20,000 years ago during the latter stages of the last Ice Age, or Pleistocene. In the last glacial period, North America was home to a set of mammals wholly different from that of today. Among them were mammoth, rhinoceros, musk oxen, saber-tooth tigers, dire wolves, and camelids. These large animals, or megafauna, dominated the Ice Age environment. In Siberia, wandering bands hunted them using spears tipped with stone points. Archaeological evidence suggests that these same hunters then appeared in North America sometime around 15,000 years ago, although this date is still in question.

At the height of the last Ice Age, when much water was locked in glaciers, a land bridge formed between Alaska and Siberia. Never covered with ice, this now-submerged land known as Beringia was a grass tundra and home for wandering herds of megafauna. The small hunting bands following these herds walked to a new continent without realizing the significance (or getting their feet wet). They did recognize that the game was plentiful and unafraid of human predators. Human population rose dramatically, and the first Americans spread into North and South America within a few thousand years. Known as Paleo-Indians, they were the ancestors of the Mound Builders, the Aztecs, the Inca, and all Native Americans.

Bill first told me in the bamboo classroom, and periodically thereafter, that no archaeologist should become so entrenched in a particular theoretical position or model that his or her whole life is spent trying to defend it. The key to making a lifelong contribution as an archaeologist is the ability to process new information and to adapt to changes in the discipline, sort of like a successful hunter-gatherer. At the Vernon field camp in northeastern Arizona, Bill received the same wisdom from Paul Martin, who embraced the revolution in archaeology at the end of his career in the late 1960s and early 1970s when many of his contemporaries resisted. Change now seems to be the norm in archaeological method and theory. It now must accommodate a range from hard scientific approaches with similarities to chemistry and physics to the decidedly antiscientific approaches more common to recent trends in literary criticism. Most archaeologists see themselves somewhere in the middle and continue to analyze their sherds, stone tools, and broken-down buildings seeking to reconstruct past behavior. We are now in a post-New Archaeology era where the failings of the approach first advocated by Binford and Longacre are being exposed while the majority of archaeologists continue to operate within the New Archaeology paradigm.

Where the New Archaeology has come up particularly short is in its over-emphasis on environment and ecology while ignoring symbolic and ideological aspects of the past. Yet its lasting legacy can be summed in one word: optimism. Optimism that archaeology can investigate anything in the past—based on material culture—that a cultural anthropologist can study in contemporary people. As a behavioral archaeologist I share this optimism that archaeology can and should investigate gender, power, and ritual, in addition to diet, demography, and the environment, but at the same time it should strive to ensure that these reconstructions are tied to the material realities of the archaeological record.

Behavioral archaeology is the study of the relationships between human behavior and material culture (artifacts) at any time or any place. Human behavior is the activity of everyday life from eating dinner and making tools to building a bridge or waging war. Humans are unique in that all of our behaviors from the simplest to the most complex involve material culture or artifacts. We bathe in an environment of artifacts. The good thing for the archaeologist is that not only do all activities involve artifacts, but the relationships between artifacts and activities are patterned. If this were not so, and the relationship between people and things were random, then archaeology would be impossible.

Consider the homes we live in, the clothes we wear, the cars we drive, the trash we throw away and whether they reflect who we are. From these artifacts alone, an archaeologist could determine someone's job, income, marital status, hobbies, religion, and more. In fact, Bill Rathje, a "garbologist," has made a career out of reconstructing human behavior from people's trash. Trained as a Maya archaeologist, Rathje realized that a lot of archaeology involved investigating a society's garbage and that an effective field project could be run cheaper in an American landfill than at a site in the Guatemalan jungle. Since the mid-1970s he has studied household behavior based on material remains—the kind of thing dragged to the curb every week.

A lot of researchers, not just archaeologists, are curious about household consumption, but Rathje has demonstrated that examining people's trash is the best way to understand what goes on behind closed doors (in homes more substantial and less proximate than those of the Kalinga). Why not just ask folks? Researchers do conduct surveys but these data are often flawed because the residents either do not remember (How many ounces of meat did you consume in the past seven days?) or they are unwilling to tell the truth. The latter is especially evident when it comes to sweets and alcohol. Americans seem barely able to admit some things to themselves and are less than forthright about how much candy or beer they consume. Twinkie wrappers and empty Budweiser cans do not lie.

The pottery-use alteration study I conducted in Guina-ang is also behavioral archaeology. By pestering the Guina-ang women and collecting their used pots, I was laying the groundwork for a comprehensive investigation of the relationship between pottery-use activities and the resultant traces. The project, overall, was a success. My dissertation, which quickly became a book, illustrated how archaeologists can link the traces of use on their prehistoric vessels (carbon deposits, organic residue, and attrition) to specific behaviors.

In a more recent pottery-use alteration study drawing on my Kalinga work, I considered the origins of pottery on the Colorado Plateau. Despite the great popularity of sites such as Chaco Canyon,

Mesa Verde, and Canyon De Chelly, and the fact that the descendants of the ancient Puebloans—the Hopi, Zuni, and Rio Grande Pueblo groups—are well known for their beautiful pottery, very little is known about the origins of this essential technology. I sought some answers together with Eric Blinman of the Museum of New Mexico.

The earliest known pottery in the region is a polished brownware that dates to about A.D. 200. Most of these vessels are squat, neckless jars, referred to as seed jars in the Southwest. These early potters were living in pit houses, probably residing in at least two different locations during the year depending on the season, and subsisting by hunting and gathering supplemented with domesticated corn, which was introduced from Mesoamerica not long before the first pottery. What were they using the vessels for?

We examined pots from two sites, Sivu'ovi and Flattop, located in the Petrified National Forest, northeast Arizona. By examining whole or nearly whole vessels it was evident that they were used for a variety of tasks, but the most interesting find was that some of the vessels were used for cooking and not just storage. Based upon the interior carbon deposits alone, it was clear that the pots were employed in both a wet mode (boiling) and a dry mode (roasting or warming). Organic matter begins to carbonize at about 300 degrees C. If you boil food, the temperature of the interior vessel wall will never exceed 100 degrees C and no carbonization will occur. At the water line, however, floating food particles adhere to the vessel wall and carbonize because the surface temperature just above the water will exceed 300 C. In the case of the roasting or warming pots (dry mode), little or no water is present while the contents are heated, thus there is carbonization over the entire interior surface. What were the first potters on the Colorado Plateau using their vessels for? The use-alteration analysis demonstrated that some of the vessels were used to cook food over a fire, while the lack of carbonization in others suggested those were used to store or process food.

The design of pots themselves also lent credence to the idea of multiple use. Round vessels, or vessels that approach round, are the strongest possible design. These pots are very resistant to impact

Early pottery from the Colorado Plateau. This polished, globular jar dates to A.D. 200. (James Skibo)

breakage and would be the best design for a strong pot that could survive transport and rough handling. And round design, thin walls, and large amounts of temper (sand) added to the clay create a very strong cooking pot.

Cooking pots worldwide never last more than several months because of the thermal stresses when they are repeatedly placed over a fire. Thermal shock causes small cracks in the vessel that will eventually grow and render the pot unusable. A vessel with lots of mineral temper, like these vessels, tolerates thermal shock well because the small grains of sand interrupt the micro-cracks and keep the vessel from breaking in two. The round bottom is also stronger than a flat-bottomed pot, and a thin wall reduces thermal shock and makes for a vessel that is more likely to survive the tortures of an open fire.

Another important facet of behavioral archaeology is the study of how sites form. Not all archaeological sites are like Pompeii. We cannot simply brush away the dirt and find a day in prehistoric life

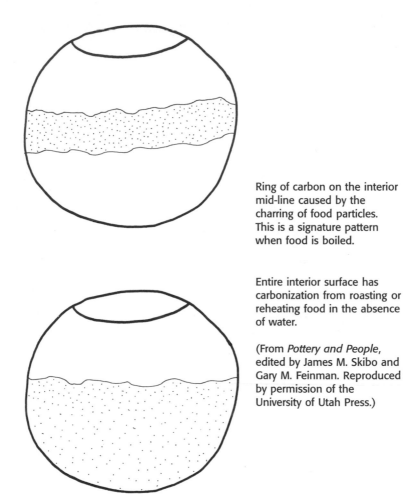

Ring of carbon on the interior mid-line caused by the charring of food particles. This is a signature pattern when food is boiled.

Entire interior surface has carbonization from roasting or reheating food in the absence of water.

(From *Pottery and People,* edited by James M. Skibo and Gary M. Feinman. Reproduced by permission of the University of Utah Press.)

frozen in time. Behavioral archaeologists in particular spend a good deal of time reconstructing formation processes, the whole series of human and environmental factors that transform the artifacts of everyday life into the objects archaeologists finally excavate and analyze.

In contrast to behavioral archaeology, which as an unbiased participant I believe is completely open-minded and the best approach to understanding many aspects of past life once thought to be inaccessible, there is a hyper-relativist archaeology. At the risk of sounding like a curmudgeon, I admit its positions intolerable. Influenced by postmodernism, it suggests that science, including archaeology, is bunk. Rather, reconstructions of the prehistoric past are simply aspects of an agenda to promote some archaeologist's ideology, like capitalism or colonialism. Admittedly, we are all captives of our own culture, meaning there is no such thing as a completely objective archaeology. There are still good examples of archaeology employed for overt political ends, and archaeologists are as capable of being racist or fascist as the next person. Yet archaeology, like all of science, is not just a set of facts but a series of well-reasoned arguments. Thus, if our arguments are clearly laid out with supporting evidence for all to see, then others can evaluate our reconstructions and possibly see through our cultural biases, whatever they may be.

While professionals will bicker about theory, we sometimes forget that what justifies archaeology is our innate curiosity about what came before. Archaeology can also offer some lessons from the past. We cannot predict the future with certainty, but we can make forecasts based on observing four million years of human adaptation and change. One prediction we can make from an archaeological perspective is the collapse of our civilization. When I teach about the rise and fall of civilizations, students sometimes inquire about the fate of the United States, currently the most powerful nation on earth. Will it also fall like Rome, the Maya, or Cahokia? Civilizations, or state-level organizations with a standing army, complex bureaucracy, tax collection, and a powerful centralized government, have come and gone dozens of times in the history of the world. There is wide variation in the size and organizational structure of these states, but in the end they shared one thing—they collapsed.

Some scholars take an even wider perspective to consider the extinction of our human species as a whole. In their provocative book, *The Sixth Extinction*, Richard Leakey and Roger Lewin discuss the five great extinctions in the 530 million years since life first appeared on this planet. The most famous of these extinctions occurred around 65 million years ago and resulted in the demise of the giant reptiles that ruled the earth with great success for millions more years than humans have been around. The likely cause for the extinction of the dinosaurs was a meteor impact on Mexico's Yucatan peninsula. The other less famous mass extinctions, when at least 65 percent of the world's species disappeared in a geologic instant, occurred at 440, 365, 225, and 210 million years ago. The extinction at the end of the Permian period (225 million years ago) was actually much more catastrophic than the dinosaur extinction because about 95 percent of marine animal species completely vanished.

Leakey, a well-known paleoanthropologist, and Lewin, a scientific journalist, argue that we already are on a slippery slope toward extinction. This time it is not because of some asteroid or through uncontrollable environmental change but through our own behavior. They believe that if we continue to destroy the world's habitat, about 50 percent of the earth's species will be extinct within the next century. This could be the beginning of the sixth great world extinction. Not only would this event be caused entirely by humans, but eventually it might include us.

Bill Longacre and I continue our discussions but now it is primarily at a distance through e-mail rather than next to a flickering oil lamp and a half-empty bottle of Collectors. We frequently ended the night in Guina-ang extolling the merits of Collectors, which we had convinced ourselves would be top-shelf whiskey anywhere in the world. Nights when the bottle neared empty we laid plans to become the North American distributors for this amazing product, thereby sharing the Philippine nectar with humanity and getting rich in the process. Our distributorship dreams are long faded, but I will never forget the lessons of the bamboo classroom.

CHAPTER 6

"Are We in Danger?"

A FEW DAYS BEFORE Becky was due to arrive, the people of Guina-ang decided to hold a village-wide celebration, a *fiesta*. It had been fifteen years since the last fiesta and the village leaders, inspired by our presence, thought it was about time. Preparation was extensive. The actual event included games, dancing, food, drinking, and even an "inspirational talk" by "Billy" Longacre, all with a surprising amount of formality. A program in English was prepared, typed at the high school, and mimeographed for the guests who could read. The schedule, followed only roughly, indicated not just the times for "parlorgames" and dancing, but also the committees and names of individuals responsible for planning the event. The program reminded me of my home-town Fourth of July celebration, though I didn't recall a list of committeemen in charge of pig butchering. I had a great time.

Bill Longacre and project members from the other villages showed up for the event. During one of the many speeches Bill pulled me aside. "We need to talk, alone." Late in the afternoon we were able to slip away relatively unnoticed from the festivities and headed for my house. This part of the village was remarkably deserted, but the sounds of the ongoing celebration could be heard clearly, serving to amplify the gravity of Bill's news. Two nights earlier a man carrying a grenade launcher had entered Bill's Dangtalan house and handed him a note that said, "Give us 20,000 pesos or we will kill you in three days." The man claimed to be a member of the New Peoples Army. More men waited outside. Bill, ever the cool negotiator, convinced them he did not have 20,000 pesos but that he would gladly give them 2,000 pesos (about 65 U.S. dollars). They seemed satisfied and Bill even got them to sign a receipt. They also told him not to tell anyone on pain of death. Bill had not told any of the Kalinga assistants. We found out later the NPA claim was false, but Bill was certain that this was just the beginning of problems with holduppers and that it would be best to be prepared for departure. Another visit from the holduppers would be reason to leave as soon as possible.

We returned to the fiesta but my exuberant mood had been doused. Although I danced, sang, and drank *basi* until about two in the morning, my mind was elsewhere. I went back to the house and stayed up until dawn working out a plan to complete the project in less time than originally scheduled. Bill had already arranged to have two hundred new pots from Dangtalan transported to Guina-ang for exchange with the old pots, my research collection. While the celebration continued until first light, I mapped out what needed to be done to enable a hasty exit from the Pasil Valley.

Four days prior to Becky's arrival in Manila, I retraced the steps that had brought me to Guina-ang three months earlier. Bill accompanied me. His mother had just died, and although the funeral had taken place he learned through family friends that his father was not doing well. With our half-hearted encouragement, he made the trip back to Houghton, Michigan. His final instructions were, "If you get another visit from the holduppers, leave immediately." Because of the three-week lag in mail delivery, I was unable to alert Becky to the most recent difficulties.

One problem with marrying an archaeologist is that the work can require extended absences. I am not sure if anyone has bothered to keep statistics, but I have a hunch that anthropologists have a much higher divorce rate than the 50 percent national average (Margaret Mead alone had several husbands). Before beginning the project I figured this was due to the months apart. By the end I knew that simply dragging one's spouse to an obscure corner of the globe while friends remain pool-side sipping iced tea can also be grounds for divorce. On Friday, Becky was teaching thirty first-graders in a school in the upscale foothills of Tucson; the following Monday she was hitching up her pants to cross a flooded, sewage-filled street to reach our room in the Adriatico Pension House. During our short stay in Manila we walked hand-in-hand through Rizal Park, Intramauro, and other Manila landmarks, stopping for leisurely meals to catch up on each other's news. One morning we were walking to breakfast in the Ermita district when a foot-long rat hit the ground with a thud just a step ahead of us. After looking up to see if more were on the way, we stepped over the twitching rodent. I am not a believer in omens, but the black rat dying at our feet began a series of suspenseful events over the next month.

On the trip into the mountains we caught up with Bill's primary assistant, Roberto, in Tuguegarao, where we stayed overnight in the tricie capital of the Philippines. From there the ride was uneventful, but in Tabuk we heard news of two jeepney holdups in the past two days between Tabuk and Dangtalan. I was carrying 60,000 pesos for the last month's payroll and expenses, worth about $3,000 (U.S.) at the time and equivalent to four years' wages for the average Philippine laborer. We decided to wait a day before the last leg of the journey and stayed the night in Roberto's Tabuk home, a luxury even for the wealthiest Kalinga residents. We were careful to cover ourselves with the mosquito net while we slept because this was where the Guina-ang residents typically contracted malaria.

The next morning we heard nothing more of holdups along the trail, so we purchased some last-minute supplies and hopped aboard a jeepney for the slow, twisting journey into the mountains. Just outside of Tabuk, Roberto saw a roadside peddler selling fifteen-inch-tall fruit bats and yelled for the driver to stop. He bought several for his family in Dangtalan. Of course without refrigeration, the best way to purchase and preserve meat is live, and these bats, bound tightly, still clung to life. As the only available space on the crowded jeepney was at our feet, we got a good view of the animals flopping against our ankles in a valiant but futile effort to escape. Mercifully, the bats played themselves out and died one by one an hour into the journey.

On the slow ascent into the Cordillera Mountains, I escaped the choking dust again by climbing on top of the jeepney. From my vantage I was the first passenger to see another jeepney careening down the mountain. Coming abreast, the vehicles stopped and the other driver immediately began shouting. I climbed down next to Roberto who was listening attentively.

"What is he saying?" I asked.

"There is an NPA checkpoint just up the road, and they are stopping all the jeepnies." He listened further, then continued, "And this driver did not stop at the checkpoint—he drove right past and they shot at him."

"Are we going to turn around?" I asked hopefully. I was not thrilled about confronting them, knowing the NPA had kidnaped Americans on previous occasions.

"Our driver has decided to go through the checkpoint," Roberto said.

"Is this safe?"

"I don't know, I think so."

"We should go back," I insisted.

"The driver decides," was his only response.

Jeepney drivers were a bit like wagon drivers from Wild West movies. They risked their lives on a daily basis confronting holduppers and armed men from various insurgent groups and were also easy targets for villages seeking revenge in the tribal blood feud. Their services were usually available to the highest bidder. One day they would be hauling government troops and the next it might be guns for the NPA.

According to Roberto the checkpoint was to ensure that the drivers were not hauling guns for government troops. It seemed the driver who ran the checkpoint was carrying something he preferred the NPA didn't see. He was less concerned for his passengers, mostly women and high-school-age kids, who nonetheless had not sustained injury from the automatic weapons fire. I squeezed into the jeepney next to Becky and the dead bats as the driver proceeded with confidence.

Everyone grew tense as we neared the checkpoint. Rounding a corner I saw my first NPA soldier on a ridge overlooking the road. Then I saw several others dressed in camouflage and carrying automatic weapons. They were so young that they looked like kids playing war, which only increased my unease. We stopped in a small clearing where two men ordered us out of the vehicle. Another jeepney was there and we could hear a third winding down the mountain. I glanced at Becky feeling terrible for dragging her into such a mess, but she seemed calmer than I. As we were escorted to the edge of the clearing, I thought I would grab her hand and break for the jungle when the shooting started. I whispered to Roberto, "Are we in danger?"

"I don't know, I don't think so." The NPA soldiers in the clearing were older and more confident-looking than those along the road. They wore their hair longer than was typical, and from their physical appearance I guessed that they were from the Mountain Province but probably not Kalinga. Two men emptied the jeepney of all our supplies and went through everything carefully. I watched with trepidation as they got to my backpack, where the 60,000 pesos hid in a shoe at the bottom. Out went all the clothes. One soldier picked up my size-twelve Nikes and extracted the roll of bills. I was certain they would now call me aside (who else could own those shoes?) and demand immediate explanation. Certainly the Dangtalan payroll wouldn't be met. But to my amazement, he replaced the bills without comment and stuffed my possessions back into the bag.

Search complete, the obvious leader of the cadre stood in front of our huddled mass and gave us an angry exhortation. By now there were three jeepnies in the clearing. I stood in back, still figuring escape contingencies, and asked Roberto what he was saying. "He is telling the jeepney drivers that they will be killed if they are found carrying weapons or government soldiers," Roberto said from the corner of his mouth. I was relieved to learn that the drivers were the focus and that the NPA was not interested in hostages that day.

After a twenty-minute harangue, we were ordered back in our jeepney and sent on our way. Later I told Edita and Nancy, our data-recording assistants, about the incident. They were unsurprised that the NPA had returned the money, asserting the group maintained a strict code of behavior for themselves and for the people of the Mountain Province. Establishing a checkpoint that day they sought to intimidate the jeepney drivers as well as put an end to the rash of trail holdups. The Kalinga, in fact, appreciated a strong NPA presence. The vigilante justice most likely did reduce the number of robberies, as it was not uncommon for the NPA to execute highwaymen.

We finally made the last turn on the trail and took in the magnificent panorama of the Pasil Valley. For me it was a joy to see this land again, and I looked forward to returning to my work. But first we needed to introduce Becky to the people of Dangtalan, which meant multiple *miriandas* and dinners that day, concluding with dinner at Roberto's house and a fine entree of boiled bat.

The days after we returned to Guina-ang were uneventful. I started to believe that the holdupper troubles were over and that our rapid-exit plan was simply the product of paranoia.

Now I was a husband again and quickly realized that Becky and I must adopt the Kalinga style of marital behavior. Like many American couples, we were openly affectionate—something never seen among the Kalinga. It had taken me some time to determine marriage partners in Guina-ang since married men and women were rarely together. I do not recall seeing one act of affection between a married couple; no kissing or holding hands, never a pat on the back, or even a knowing smile. The Kalinga did not find anything wrong with intimate contact. Walking through the village I was likely to see two people holding hands, and in public gatherings adults would sit close to one another often with their arms wrapped around each other's neck or knees. But in every case such open displays of affection were between people of the same sex. Put ten Kalinga male friends together in a big room, and you would probably find them sitting in an interlocked mass.

Because I had been enculturated in a rather homophobic American society, it took time to get used to the sight of embracing males or adult women holding hands. Consider, however, that there is nothing about these sorts of relationships that is determined by our genetic code—we are not hard-wired to treat our spouses a certain way or refrain from snuggling our best male friend. The behaviors associated with our sexuality are determined by our culture, and there is a tremendous amount of variation worldwide. In fact, there are few obvious universals regarding sexual behavior beyond those determined by biology and reproduction. One exception would be the incest taboo; all cultures have a prohibition against having sex with one's relatives. Of course who is a relative is also culturally defined. Beyond this notable exception, what one culture might view as normal sexual relations another might label weird or bizarre.

Americans like to think of themselves as sexually enlightened, yet the evidence is otherwise. Open discussions of practices such as homosexuality, masturbation, and especially bestiality are taboo. Even the most inveterate gossips probably never talk about people having sex with animals, yet this is not an uncommon practice among pastoralists and rural people worldwide. A mid-twentieth-century survey found that over 40 percent of rural American boys admitted to having had sex with farm animals. To demonstrate the taboos regarding bestiality, consider syphilis, the common venereal disease. In my simple desk dictionary, syphilis is defined without mention of the fact that it arose through human-animal sexual contact.

One of the most extreme sexual behaviors, from my perspective, is reported by anthropologist Gilbert Herdt, who helps us understand the difference between homosexual orientation and homosexual acts. Among a horticultural group from New Guinea known as the Sambia, homosexual contacts are part of the male initiation period during which heterosexual sex is strictly prohibited. Although the Sambia clearly understand that procreation occurs because of heterosexual genital to genital contact (I need to be specific here), other forms of semen transfer are believed to be equally important. Semen is considered a scarce resource that can be passed from person to person without changing its essence. Thus, it is thought that the oral transmission of semen between a husband and wife finishes the growth of the wife and becomes mother's milk. Semen is also transferred from young to older initiates through oral sex, which they feel is a type of "male breast-feeding."

An equally fascinating behavior is the *berdache*, which was widely known among native North Americans. In the 113 groups where this practice was documented, the berdache was usually a male who assumed the dress, occupation, and behavior associated with females (the opposite did also occur occasionally). Male berdaches, who in our culture would be scorned as transvestites, often had high status and their work as women was so valued that men sought them as marriage partners. Among the Crow, for example, berdaches had the largest lodges and were considered the best seamstresses and cooks.

A final form of sexual behavior that most Westerners find perplexing is genital mutilation (despite the continuing American practice of removing the foreskins from male babies without medical cause). One of my personal favorites is the penis pin, found in Southeast Asia and even in some traditional cultures of the Philippines. The simplest form looks like a tiny barbell, one to two inches in length, that is inserted crosswise through the head of the penis. Installation requires minor surgery, but the device supposedly increases male sexual prowess and enhances female sexual pleasure. In some cultures the penis pin is also an indicator of social status. To perform this surgery (male readers cross legs now), a clamp is placed on the penis to reduce bleeding and to anesthetize the area through which a pointed shaft is driven. Some cultures also believe that standing in water reduces the pain, but because the procedure is often performed during male initiation rites, pain alleviation is not a primary concern. Given the wide arc of possible sexual behaviors, Becky and I considered ourselves quite lucky to be among the Kalinga.

Everyone wanted to get a look at Becky, and our first day in Guina-ang was draining. The crowd around us was much like my first day several months before. Exhausted by the day's events, we crawled into bed right after sundown, lulled by the patter of rats on the roof. The rats owned the night and were one of the most difficult things to get used to in Guina-ang. It was especially unsettling in a better-appointed home such as ours, which had a corrugated steel roof that amplified the sounds of rodent to-and-fro. It was like living in a metal drum. Even worse was when the roof-running ceased, at which point it was fairly certain a foray into the house had begun. The late-night boozing with my Kalinga age-mates usually caused me to sleep through the rat noises, but it was still slightly unnerving to find rat droppings around my bed in the morning. I asked my assistants if it bothered them and they all said they hated the rats. "Why not get a cat?" I asked one morning. Although it would take a tough cat to handle the big jungle rats, the solution seemed obvious.

"Someone had a cat once," replied one assistant, "but it did not last too long because somebody ate it." They went on to explain that poison seemed to be effective and people did occasionally buy rat poison in Tabuk. So on the trip back to Guina-ang I had brought a package of poison "guaranteed to kill hundreds of rats." I hoped to spare Becky the nightly ordeal of trying to fall asleep during the rat patrol. But that night we went to bed without unpacking our half dozen bags of supplies. Lying there we listened to the rats dancing on the roof and then rummaging through our supplies. Too exhausted to care, we fell asleep quickly and slept through the night. The next morning I went through the supplies myself and found that our guests had eaten through a bottle of shampoo, causing it to leak onto the floor. The reality of an anticipated luxury denied reminded me of the rat poison, and I searched until I found what was left. It appeared that a single rat had chewed its way into this bag and consumed enough poison to "kill hundreds of rats." Somewhere in the rafters there was one really dead rat.

All of my assistants strongly recommended that I hold a village-wide *palanos* to welcome Becky. Failure to do so would be very shameful for me, they said. Doing it right required a pig and a large jar (five gallons or more) of *basi*. I knew I was being manipulated but I thought it would be fun. That morning, I asked my assistants to buy enough *basi* and a pig substantial enough that I would not bring shame upon myself. Early in the afternoon they returned from Lubuagon, a difficult several-hour hike, carrying a squealing pig. They butchered it, cut it into hundreds of pieces, put the meat in a caldron of boiling water, and by nightfall the party was under way. The entire population of Guina-ang, five hundred or more, assembled in a plaza for what turned out to be an agreeable night of singing, dancing, eating, and drinking. Having been to my share of Polish-style weddings, I felt quite comfortable with this celebration. The men played gongs, the women danced, speeches were made, I sang my usual *salidomy*, and took my turn playing the gongs.

Salidomys came in many variations, but they typically had a repeating melody followed by an original verse to suit the occasion.

My rendition, awful as it was, seemed to be appreciated even if it did not approach the melodic and poetic *salidomys* sung that night by vastly more talented Kalinga. The highlight of the night was the courtship dance (*solidseed*), which they insisted that Becky and I dance so that we could be married "Kalinga style." Becky was dressed in the traditional skirt (*tapice*) and beads to prepare her for the two-person dance. Since Becky and I had no idea how to go about things, several Guina-ang residents served as our instructors and guides; we had only to mimic their movements. Solono and I carried a *tapice* and chased Becky and her escort around the plaza to the beat of the gongs and the almost deafening laughter of the children. The party broke up only when all the wine was consumed, well into the early morning hours.

Formerly, traditional Kalinga marriages were arranged by parents, to the extent that a boy and girl could be engaged soon after birth. As in other parts of the world, such practices were growing less common, though at one time they were the standard form of marital union. That is because in many societies marriage, until very recently, has been more of an economic and political transaction than a consummation of romantic love. Westerners now find the mere thought of arranged marriages repulsive, but just several generations ago many Americans of Italian, Polish, and Greek heritage, for example, followed this practice. In fact, in some ethnic neighborhoods of American cities, arranged marriages continue to this day, and, surprisingly or not, the divorce rate is lower than for marriages in which individuals choose their partners. A marriage that involves the transfer of money, land, or political and social connections is much more difficult to dissolve than one based on romantic love or infatuation. Marriage in most non-Western cultures is a union of two families, not simply an agreement between a man and woman—as we like to tell ourselves.

Among the Kalinga, families would exchange gifts several times during the engagement, which itself could go on for years. At the days-long wedding ceremony, gift giving had an air of competition as a family stood to gain status and prestige for its generosity. The newlyweds often received a share of their inheritance, including rice fields, carabaos, Chinese jars, and gold jewelry. In many tradi-

Children assembled for our *palanos*, or welcome party. (James Skibo)

tional, non-Western societies, the family created by marriage is the primary economic unit. There is a distinct division of labor between the husband and wife, each performing tasks important to the family's survival. Among the Kalinga, for example, the planting, harvesting, rice processing, and tending of swidden gardens required the active participation of both husband and wife.

In many societies the preferred marriage is between cousins, which I was assured as a youngster would probably produce children with three arms or worse. Some harmful effects can be caused by continual inbreeding because of the reappearance of recessive genes (a good example is the frequency of hemophiliacs among Queen Elizabeth's descent line), but in most cases cousin marriage is harmless.

The incest taboo has long fascinated anthropologists because it is a cultural universal—all societies have rules that prohibit sex among close family members. Minimally, this includes sex between parents and children and sex between siblings, yet almost all societies extend the taboo to others. For example, in many societies some cousins are acceptable mates while others are considered siblings. There is a wide range of explanations, from genetic to psychological to

Kalinga villagers dancing with gongs and wearing traditional clothing. (James Skibo)

cultural for the universal incest taboo. One line of reasoning is that an abhorrence for incest is genetically wired. Support for this can be found among our fellow primates, the monkeys and apes. To avoid incestuous unions, adolescent male monkeys and female apes leave their group. Thus, it is possible that humans have an instinctive horror of incest and created a variety of cultural rules and laws in response. Anthropology, however, typically rejects most explanations that rely too heavily on genetic wiring or psychology and instead seeks cultural and social causes for such things.

For hunter-gatherers, the only human adaptation until about 10,000 years ago, there are two important cultural benefits of the incest taboo. First, marrying outside a small group of fifty or fewer (the typical size for a hunting-and-gathering band) increases the group's chances for survival. Sending daughters and sons away at marriage to live with another group creates alliances with neighbors and promotes friendly relations that can be counted on during times of food stress. A second cultural explanation is that permitting sexual unions within a small group creates disharmony between blood family members who depend upon one another for

Becky attempting the courtship dance with Delia Sawil. (James Skibo)

survival. For example, in hunting-and-gathering bands, all decisions are made as a whole and all food is shared equally.

The Kalinga, fortunately, did not have to worry about finding me a marital partner, but they were concerned about our lack of children. No doubt this was the the subject of much discussion because we heard almost every day from a different person that "you must drink from Kaboníyan Spring." Kaboníyan Spring, or God's Spring, was an artesian well flowing from a cliff just outside Guina-ang. According to one and all, a drink from its waters was a cure for infertility (always the female's fault). Divorce was uncommon in Kalinga, but when it did occur a woman's infertility was usually cited. I knew of a Guina-ang man who divorced his wife for this reason and then married a woman who also turned out to be barren. The Kalinga considered this a case of simple bad luck.

To avoid further badgering, Becky and I agreed that a visit to the magical waters of Kaboníyan Spring was indeed necessary. We climbed the trail to the spring, which was flowing miraculously from the mountainside. Becky took a long drink in front of several witnesses. Fifteen months later our first child was born.

A drink from Kaboníyan Spring is certain to increase fertility. (James Skibo)

Of course our child was born in a sterile hospital birthing room complete with a birthing bed, a fetal heart monitor, and other devices now considered requisite for a North American birth, plus a bathroom and TV for our convenience. But just a century ago childbirth was the leading cause of death among young women and in the absence of medical intervention can still be quite dangerous. The Kalinga now have midwives who have received some medical training, but traditionally only the mother and other close relatives assisted. Kalinga women give birth at home. At the onset of labor someone suspends a rope from the rafters. The expectant mother pulls on the rope while relatives knead and press her belly. The child is received by the woman's mother, who cuts the cord with a bamboo knife and then washes the baby in soft bark.

On May 18, Christopher Turner, one of the Dangtalan researchers, appeared at our Guina-ang doorstep with more disturbing news. The previous day Brian and Chris had received a note demanding seven thousand pesos. They were instructed to bring the cash to an isolated spot where the holduppers would meet them under cover of darkness. Following Bill's example, they decided to give only two thousand pesos. One of their assistants insisted on transferring the money himself. After the delivery their assistant said he recognized one of the men and that they were not NPA, just thugs from Ableg, the village just below Dalupa. Chris said he and Brian intended to leave in the next several days. We too set our plan in motion. Of course the midnight payoff was soon common knowledge and our village buzzed with the news. Amboy learned that the Guina-ang anthropologists were also going to get a visit, now that it was known that Bill was not the only researcher with access to large amounts of cash.

CHAPTER 7

What Goes in Must Come Out

"IT HAS BEEN a difficult two days," I wrote in my journal on Monday, May twenty-third. I had spent them battling intestinal problems and high fever. Returning from Dangtalan the previous Saturday I had begun to feel ill. By nighttime I had diarrhea. Becky thought it was stress, which was possible given recent events.

We had stayed in Dangtalan overnight to discuss our group's run-ins with holduppers and now an outbreak of tribal war. Despite the end of headhunting, blood feuds continued. Tensions between nearby villages had erupted into violence and we could hear distant gunshots occasionally. It seemed that a small group of men was now shooting at random into the village of Ableg from a nearby hill. Bill's departing words hung over us all. It was definitely time to go. I hoped my stomach distress was due simply to the absence of our leader, but the simple case of L.B.M., as my mother once called it, was the beginning of intestinal problems that plagued me for months.

Though I possessed powerful medication to prevent the immediate danger, extreme dehydration, I passed the night with alternating episodes of chills and sweats. I felt better the next morning, so I decided to proceed with my research routine. After lunch I dragged home, stomach twisted in knots, head bursting, with skin that was hot even to my own touch. I had no way of knowing my temperature, but it was the hottest I have ever felt. Becky convinced me to take a cold shower (which, of course, was the only option) but it had little effect.

The afternoon and the rest of the night I was in a feverish fog. Becky kept cool towels on me through the night, and she was suddenly in charge of dispensing medicine to supplicants and running the project. She held things together, though she confessed in her own journal entry for that day, "I have never been so afraid." During periods of seeming lucidity I tried to focus on the possibility of being carried out of Guina-ang along with my two hundred pots. Becky told me later that Amboy stopped in occasionally to check on me and to discuss the procedure step-by-step for getting me to a hospital. Had my condition not improved, Amboy would have arranged for the Kalinga ambulance—a bamboo stretcher carried by the young men. I decided it was malaria. I had seen several Guina-ang residents gripped by similar agony, but each had recovered fully after a course of medication.

My fever broke early the following morning, suggesting that I did not have malaria after all. The intestinal problems continued unabated, however. We had reached the final days of the project, and I needed to stay on my feet. Eating anti-diarrhea pills, I could get some work done, but I felt weaker each day and was never without a dull headache. Diarrhea was suddenly the least of my problems. Still, I was thankful that the holduppers had at least waited long enough for us to conclude most of our research. All that remained was to pack pots and arrange for shipment to Manila.

Packing up pots required hundreds of hours of labor. We began by wrapping them in a Goretex material with a Teflon-like coating on one side. Because my research involved the study of the use-alteration traces on the vessels, we did not want anything to be added or lost during the long journey back to Tucson. The Goretex came in four-foot-wide rolls and was difficult to keep in place. Some experimentation before the fieldwork began and consultation with experts in artifact curation and transport determined that queen-size, control-top B pantyhose was the answer. We cut the pantyhose unmercifully into sections with the toes and legs for the small pots and the thigh and upper section for the larger vessels. If the Guina-ang residents did not think we were strange by then, the pot wrapping banished any remaining doubts. The women of the village

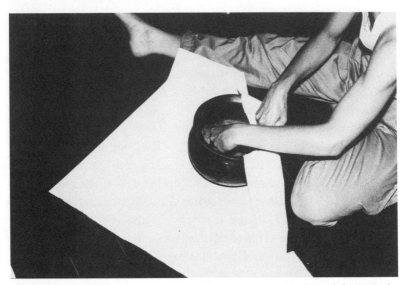

Wrapping pots to preserve their surfaces for transport to Manila and the United States (James Skibo)

visited in small groups to watch. One minute their old pots were virtually worthless cookware and then the pots were given treatment more proper to sacred relics. The women huddled with my female assistants with much whispering, giggling, and head shaking.

After the layers of Goretex and pantyhose, we finished with a more traditional packaging material. Our male assistants went to the forest to cut soft, spongy banana bark and hauled it back to the village in large bundles. We then stacked four pots or so with small pieces of bark between them. The entire bundle we wrapped with long pieces of banana bark and strapped securely with rattan. The result was a torpedo-shaped bundle that was easy to carry yet remarkably protective. I did find some breakage when I opened the shipment back in Tucson, but all the pots survived their bumpy journey to Manila. Unfortunately, the banana bark had to be removed in Manila because of U.S. Customs restrictions regarding the transport of organic material. I suspect that if the pots had been left in their cocoons instead of being repacked in crates all would have survived.

Study pots in various stages of collection and packing. The new pots on the left are being exchanged for worn pots; pots in the center are wrapped first in Goretex and pantyhose; and the vessels on the far right are stacked, wrapped in banana bark, and ready for transport. (James Skibo)

At 5:30 in the morning on May twenty-third our pots began riding off on the heads of women to the nearest road in Ableg. Because custom prohibited men from hauling pots, we hired women to make the day long round trip. Several days before, we had spread the word that we were seeking all available women to carry more than fifty pot bundles down the trail. The first woman in line that morning, however, would not accept payment from our assistants. This was the woman I had first seen several months earlier curled in a fetal position and wracked with malarial fever. I had sent her to the hospital and now she was better, feeling strong, and overjoyed at the possibility of repayment. It was gratifying to see this sturdy woman on her feet again and leading the convoy of carriers. One by one they balanced the loads on their heads and joined the growing line.

Amboy and Becky did most of the arranging for packing day and the first day of transport. I was growing weaker by the hour and spent my time on the porch watching their minute-to-minute

Stacking the wrapped pots for transport. (James Skibo)

Wrapping pots in banana bark and rattan. (Reprinted by permission of the Arizona State Museum, William Longacre photo)

A Guina-ang woman beginning the half-day walk to Ableg carrying a bundle of study pots on her head. (James Skibo)

supervising. Becky had also packed our personal belongings in secret, because only she and I knew that tomorrow we too would be leaving. I composed a letter to the village leaders explaining the reasons for our hasty departure.

The next morning we woke early and told our landlords and assistants of our plans. Because of the holdupper gossip, they understood completely the need to leave without fanfare. The Kalinga love a big send-off party, yet the fact that nobody suggested one underscored the seriousness of the threat. I hoped the villagers would not feel insulted, but they seemed both relieved about our safety and happy to be absolved of responsibility. We gathered our belongings and joined the day's group of about twenty-five women carrying the remaining pots to Ableg. The plan was to meet a National Museum truck there, load up, and ride back to Manila. I had never been to Ableg, the supposed home of our holduppers, nor was I sure my guts would cooperate for the trip. It turned out to be a beautifully clear day, and the downhill trail provided many opportunities for spectacular overlooks of the Pasil River Valley. Because we were near the end of the pot carriers, we could watch their long line snaking down the steep switchbacks.

Twenty minutes into our walk we met a Guina-ang man who held the largely ceremonial position of Chief of Police in the Pasil Valley. One of his responsibilities was to listen to a morning radio broadcast that carried Kalinga-Apayao news and bulletins. He approached me and said, "Guina-ang Skibo, the National Museum truck will not be arriving today." By now I was accustomed to the unpredictability of life in the valley, but this was still disturbing. Our carefully laid plans had been foiled. I conferred with Becky and my assistants. We agreed it would be safest to spend the night in Guina-ang and then head for Ableg in the morning in the hope that the Museum vehicle had been delayed just one day. It was hard to see my precious pots marching down the valley to the stronghold of the holduppers without me.

Nearing Guina-ang I suggested that we spend the day outside of the village, despite my intestinal mutiny. Amboy thought this was a wise idea, and we entered town only long enough to deposit our belongings at the old house. The village seemed practically deserted anyway. All the able-bodied women were carrying my pots, and most everyone else was tending fields or picking up the child-care slack created by the absent mothers. I had never traveled much north of Guina-ang, so we decided to hike farther into the mountains, not coincidentally the opposite direction of Ableg. We started on the trail to Bagtayan, which was on the border of virgin stands of coniferous trees and what the people called "the forest." People traveled here often to obtain rattan for making baskets and pine resin, which the potters used to seal their vessels after firing. Although the land around Guina-ang looked forested, it was secondary, deciduous growth, which quickly filled in after the slash-and-burn gardens were abandoned. The conifers had vanished generations ago. On the trail we met John and Deliah, Amboy's brother and sister-in-law, who joined us for the day hike. They had been inspecting their grove of coffee trees growing at the higher, cooler elevation. As we ascended the mountain, the temperature dropped noticeably. Eventually we reached the forest just outside of Bagtayan. John and Deliah wanted to take us into the village, but I knew that my guts would not tolerate the rounds of sweetened coffee and piles of sticky rice. We rested on the trail overlooking

Bagtayan and headed back to Guina-ang in the mid-afternoon in order to arrive just prior to dark.

As dusk fell we strolled into the village unnoticed, we hoped. Amboy, Joseph, and a few other male age-mates assembled at our house. Becky and I were happy for their company, thinking no holdupper would challenge the local tough guys. At first our talk was sober as we went over the day's events, holdupper problems, and a new plan for a safe exit, but then things grew more upbeat as our friends recognized the opportunity to give us a proper send-off. Some pop-bottle gin materialized, a squealing pig was hauled in, and we had a small farewell party. When they butchered the pig they cut out the liver and held it under the light of the single lantern. Huddling around the liver to read the spots, our assistants soon proclaimed that we would indeed get out safely. Taking heart, we drank and sang with enthusiasm.

A pounding gin headache compounded my weakened state as we got another early-morning start, hoping that the Museum's truck and drivers would be there. Arriving in Ableg I asked to see where our pots were stored. We found the bundles standing at attention in a small house next to the dusty road through town. The truck had not arrived, nor could anyone tell us about it. I looked around. Compared to Guina-Ang, Ableg seemed dirty and depressing. The roadside stalls that had sprouted chaotically were covered with dust from the daily jeepney arrivals. Going back to Guina-ang was no longer an option, so Becky and I chose to take the next jeepney out of the valley intending to stay the night in the Hotel Delfino in Tuguegarao. The pots would simply have to find their own way to Manila.

By the end of yet another day bouncing in the jeepney, Tuguegarao was a relief. I purchased bus tickets for the final day-long ride to Manila. But at the bus stop early the next morning we learned our ride had not only failed to arrive but would probably never show. Another bus company was a few blocks away and there we found a glorious red, air-conditioned coach due to leave for Quezon City just outside Manila in twenty minutes. I thought our luck was turning until I saw the bathroom on the bus, filled to the ceiling with boxes and luggage. My intestines gurgled in protest as we climbed aboard for an eight-hour ride with just two stops. The drugs had confined my L.B.M. to periods after eating or drinking, but I took a double-dose, wondering what it was doing to my kidneys, and did not eat for the entire trip.

The noise, dirt, and squalor of the big city was a welcome relief after the agonizing trip. Immediately upon exiting the bus we took an expensive cross-city taxi (much to the delight of the driver) to the Ermita district and our usual pension only to discover it was full. In a pouring rain we carried our bags from place to place until we found an opening at the Malate Pension, appropriately the place where I had spent my first night in Manila.

My main concern was for the pots, and we checked the warehouse daily. Finally they appeared and were unpacked by Museum personnel and crated for the sea voyage to San Francisco. The dank warehouse had once been a proud government building, built during the American Period but now in deep disrepair. Like museums worldwide, the Philippine Museum system suffered from the usual problems of under-funding and third-hand facilities. Still, the museum staff was dedicated and highly trained. It was a relief to see the pots in their hands. Even better, I was overjoyed to find the data-collection forms, representing hundreds of hours of work, which in a moment of lunacy I had packed with the pots.

The short trips to the museum and elsewhere were enabled only by bursts of energy from the electrolyte drink Becky had found somewhere. As it was, I returned to our room exhausted. Each day I thought would be a turning point in my health, but days and then weeks passed unrelieved. In the Philippines one can buy almost any medical drug without a prescription. I sampled various potent remedies intended to kill off the most common intestinal invaders without result. We had planned a week on the resort beaches, but now it seemed best to return to the States. Trying to change our existing tickets to an earlier date, we found the first available seats were on a flight two weeks hence.

Bill was supposed to be returning to Manila soon. We went to breakfast daily at our Ermita rendezvous, one of the only cafes serving brewed coffee instead of the instant variety preferred by Filipinos. One morning there sat Bill reading the paper at his usual table.

He was anxious to hear about the Pasil Valley exodus and the whereabouts of the other team members. After we had talked for an hour
about project details and his trip to the Upper Peninsula, Becky
brought up my now-perpetual medical condition. Bill had long ago
become an expert on intestinal afflictions. He inquired closely about
my symptoms and seemed concerned by what I told him; most
cases lasted several days and then cleared up. It turned out that
beyond solicitude for my well-being he had a personal interest in
the matter. In fact, he had the same symptoms. His problems began on the flight back to the Philippines, which put me a little over
a week ahead in terms of the progression of the illness. "Since you
are sicker," Bill said with authority, "you should go to the doctor."

There are two types of doctors in the Philippines: ones who
hang their shingle in the street and may or may not have any medical training, and ones who have undergone rigorous medical training at institutions comparable to the best U.S. medical schools. Bill
said I could find the good kind at the Makati Medical Center and
argued that it was silly for us both to go. One of us could identify
the exact cause and determine the proper course of treatment, while
the other could derive equal benefit. This seemed logical.

The next morning Becky and I trudged off to the Makati Medical Center, which was indeed an impressive facility. I felt better just
looking at the building, not just because I knew there might be
anwers within and an end to my self-medication, but because it was
more like our Western medical temples where "real" medicine occurs.

After filling up some forms (as they say in the Philippines), showing my credit card, and a short wait (all familiar and reassuring
rituals), I was seen by an expert in intestinal disorders. He did not
disappoint. Yet before getting around to my illness he first described
his internship in Chicago in detail, and we shared stories about
places we knew in common. Finally addressing my problem, he
announced, "It's a good thing you came to see me before going
home, because U.S. doctors would not have a clue about some of
our parasites and amoebas." I mentioned my recent adventures in
pharmacology and he smiled, shook his head, replying that while I
had surely nuked all the common stuff there were whole series of
things unfazed by such weapons. He did a quick exam and con-

cluded I was dangerously dehydrated and that if we did not solve the issue immediately he would admit me to the hospital. He gave me a cup for a stool sample, which would be no problem, but added it was quite unlikely they would find the culprit there. All my medication had probably killed off the more visible signs. I was to return the next day for a rectal wash.

A rectal wash did not sound exciting but by then I would have agreed to just about anything. I showed up early the next morning without having eaten and was shown into an examining room with a strange table at its center. I was directed to disrobe and put on the usual hospital gown split up the back. The doctor entered and told me that the next step to identifying my exact problem required a sample from the wall of my large intestine. They laid me on my stomach, restrained my hands and feet, and cranked the table so that my knees drew to my chest and my butt slowly rose to eye level. Bill's logic was crystal clear now, and I swore vengeance. The assistant started a noisy vacuum pump and the doctor picked up a wide-diameter length of hose, warning, "This is going to be quite uncomfortable, but just breathe through your nose and try to relax." Relaxing was impossible, but breathing through my nose kept me from yelling and embarrassing my stoic ancestors. "Just a little bit more," said the doctor. I wondered if the little bit more was really necessary or whether it was his small repayment for the injustices of the American Period. Probably every American who came to the Makati Medical Center got a rectal wash.

My suspicions were unfounded (I think) because the doctor said he had identified the culprit amoeba and prescribed the proper medication. He noted that the drugs would also eradicate the entire spectrum of bacteria in my digestive tract, most of which are necessary for digestion. Further, the recolonization of my system with Filipino bacteria would be unsettling and a complete cure could not be effected until I returned to the States and American (by god) bacteria. He predicted that I would begin to see some relief, but I could not expect normal digestion until I returned to the homeland and ate cultured yogurt three times a day. I did begin to feel better after several days, which gave us an opportunity to explore the city a little more.

We made trips to Intramauros, Malacanang Palace, and other Manila landmarks in wet clothes because it was now the rainy season and impossible to do tourism and remain dry. To get around the city we either took the ever-present Jeepnies or hailed cabs. Obviously we were not Filipinos and as we moved about the city, people on the street, cab drivers, or waiters occasionally inquired if we were Americans. On confession, we were often held accountable for our country and asked to explain various U.S. government policies and decisions. Months and even years go by and most Americans do not hear or think about the Philippines. But American government, entertainment, and sports news were a staple of Manila's daily papers.

On more than one occasion people asked me angrily why the Philippines was still economically stagnant while Japan was prospering. The atrocities inflicted upon Filipinos by Japanese soldiers in World War II were still a source of deep anger. It hardly seemed fair to many Filipinos that Japan, the loser, had rebounded (with America's help) so quickly and dramatically while on the winning side the Philippines languished. The bitterness was exacerbated as Japanese tourists, extremely wealthy by comparison, stayed in the best hotels or even arrived on company-sponsored sex junkets to indulge themselves in the red-light districts. Our efforts at explanation involving the relative strengths of prewar industrial bases, Korean-war-era investments, and comparisons of extractive and manufacturing economies hardly seemed adequate to agitated cab drivers and the like.

Of course the question of why some people are the conquerors and others the conquered has long interested historians and social scientists. In his book *Guns, Germs, and Steel: The Fates of Human Societies*, Jared Diamond counters the claim that there is a racial basis why, for example, it was the Filipinos who were conquered by the Japanese rather than the opposite. According to Diamond, the fate of peoples follows different courses for environmental and historical reasons, not because of any biological superiority or inferiority. Pizarro conquered 80,000 seasoned Inca soldiers with 200 conquistadors because of horses, guns, steel weapons, armor, and disease. And Europeans possessed guns, horses, and steel not because they were smarter but rather because of a whole series of factors, such as greater population and early adoption of agriculture, that put them in a position of dominance. If you are at the receiving end of European expansion and colonization, however, this may be of little consolation.

Another thing that we encountered among both the Kalinga and the people of Manila was a perception that we possessed great personal wealth. The Kalinga often told us, "You are so rich." We tried to tell them that all of our worldly possessions could fit into a car and that as graduate students we had accepted a life of poverty. But when we finally arrived in the States, dropped off by the airport taxi at our townhouse (which we rented from my in-laws for virtually nothing), and walked in the door we looked at each other and said, "We *really are* rich."

The Kalinga adventure gave us a small view of American culture from an outsider's perspective. Americans consider themselves a religious society, but to a Kalinga highlander it is clear that what we really worship is money. We are the richest society in the history of the world and equate success and happiness with material possessions. Living with people who have virtually no material wealth one discovers it is possible to be perfectly happy without all the things Westerners consider necessary. Poets and songwriters tell us money cannot buy love or happiness, yet Americans seem ever more determined to prove otherwise. We, like any people, prefer to think that our way is the best way or the correct way. Perhaps this is not always the case.

CHAPTER 8

Kalinga Justice

ONE LATE AFTERNOON Amboy and I were sitting in my house after a punishing game of Guina-ang-style basketball when we heard a disturbance from the edge of the village. Stepping out of the house we could hear the outraged voice of a man accompanied by crashing sounds, yelping dogs, and squealing pigs. I turned to Amboy, but he was already gone. Across the plaza my neighbor scurried up the steps into her house, closed the door, and peered through the window. I did not understand what the fellow was saying, but as the commotion drew closer I could tell this was one angry guy.

Suddenly, the ranting was very near and a shirtless man, fists punching the air wildly, crossed the plaza. Not only did he sound crazy with rage, but he looked it as well. A small group of young men, including Amboy, followed closely. I recognized him, a man about twenty years old who worked outside the village and whom I had seen occasionally playing basketball or visiting his mother's house just to the north of me. To avoid any potential confrontation, I followed my neighbor's lead and went into my house. Amboy and the group of young men were now trying to restrain the man but with limited result. The screaming, crashing, and howling continued for another quarter hour. Then the village went silent, and people slowly emerged from their houses to discuss the incident. I was mystified until Amboy returned looking disheveled. The man was drunk and simply "went crazy."

Kalinga men could be aggressive when drunk, and disorderly conduct was not unheard of. Young Kalinga men were more prone to such outbursts as they dealt with the mounting frustrations of living between the worlds of the traditional Kalinga and the more Westernized Filipinos. Amboy, as both he and others told me, had often exhibited similar behavior. As the youngest son of a father who owned few rice fields, Amboy could not expect to be a prosperous Kalinga rice farmer. Years later, although I have not managed to communicate with him directly, I do know he attempted to move out of the Kalinga world, but for a variety of reasons he is back in the village pursuing his old livelihood as a gold miner.

I asked Amboy how they subdued the angry man, and he said that once they finally captured him they simply removed his pants. "Works on me every time," Amboy said matter-of-factly. I had never heard of such a tactic but immediately recognized its genius. Naked from the waist down, the man went from maniacal rage to embarrassed humility and trotted back to his house trying to cover his genitals. Clearly, only someone who was insane would continue rampaging after losing his pants. This was one of numerous Kalinga methods I witnessed for dealing with social deviance. In many respects I felt their ways were more successful and humane for both victim and law-breaker than those in our society.

The Kalinga are famous among anthropologists for a complex system of peace pacts intended to resolve inter-tribal disputes without recourse to violence, but what fascinated me most was the manner in which they settled issues we divide into civil and criminal law. During my stay there was a rape and a serious theft. In each case the Kalinga *pangat* moved swiftly. I first heard of the rape of a Guina-ang woman from Edita, who told me that the brother of the victim was coming to our village that day with a gun. There was much shouting that evening between the families of the assailant and the victim, but the *pangat* from each family intervened and took charge of matters before any violence erupted. The accused had fled the village, not in an attempt to avoid punishment but on the advice of family members seeking to calm a volatile situation. The *pangat* repaired to the house of one of Guina-ang's leaders to negotiate and worked through the night and the following day. Finally the next night word came that they had reached a conclusion and were killing a pig to mark the settlement.

They invited me into the house where I found six tired but happy elderly men. As I gazed at their fatigued faces, I wondered if the resolution had been furthered by the prospect of yet another sleepless night. I sat next to one of the *pangat* who explained what had transpired. The *pangat*, as esteemed members of the community, were given tremendous latitude to resolve the case serving as both judge and jury in a trial combining criminal and civil proceedings. They had determined the guilt of the rapist and agreed on a settlement for the victim. Since this was a very serious offense, they awarded the victim several rice fields owned by the assailant's family—a huge settlement. Essentially, the victim received a good portion of the rapist's inheritance. The young girl came from a poor family with few fields; the settlement would greatly improve her family's economic standing; and the rapist sustained a tremendous and lasting financial penalty.

My friend asked me what I thought about the decision and I told him I was very impressed by the entire proceeding. Speaking to the assembled *pangat*, I told them rape was also a serious crime in my country for which rapists receive lengthy jail sentences but that the victims seemed to be treated more humanely in the Kalinga system. Aside from requiring victims to testify repeatedly and in public about the crime (thereby reducing the number of reported rape incidents), our judicial system mandates that guilt or innocence be determined by a jury of peers with no experience in the legal system and who can be manipulated by experienced trial lawyers. Compare this with the Kalinga system in which the most respected members of the community make the decisions and negotiate the settlements. This trial was concluded fewer than two days after the assault, and the victim was rewarded handsomely for her suffering. Moreover, this system also seemed better for the perpetrator: he could return to the village if he chose and resume his life, which now included working twice as hard to make up for the lost inheritance.

The Kalinga system presumed a person would not repeat the criminal activity, but what about repeat offenders? I found that the Kalinga also had a way to deal with them.

One day I was in a house conducting my pottery-use observations. About midday the man of the house appeared unexpectedly and began strapping on a bolo, speaking excitedly to his wife. At that time of year, men usually spent the entire day in the fields. From the commotion outside I knew that he was not the only one leaving his work. When I could get someone's attention I learned that a man's carabao had been stolen. In terms of economic importance, carabao were second only to rice fields and were owned only by the richest families. They were critical for tilling rice fields prior to planting. Moreover, butchered carabaos were consumed at the most important Kalinga rituals, such as funerals and weddings.

Carabao are docile animals and were simply left to graze outside the village when their services were not required. Sometimes carabao could wander, but each man knew the tracks of his animal and the animals were easily located. The owner of this carabao had gone to check the animal that morning and found it missing. He followed the tracks down the trail and concluded that the carabao was being led away by someone. Within minutes the owner had sounded the informal mountain alarm, which immediately prompted action from the men of the village.

The hastily assembled posse arrived back in the village before nightfall, having tracked the beast to the river where it had been butchered. A carabao can travel only on well-worn trails, so there were a number of witnesses. Hours after the theft, it was known that a Dalupa man was the culprit. The Kalinga considered this case more serious than the rape for two reasons. First, the thief was from Dalupa, outside Guina-ang's peace-pact. If the man had been from Galdang or Dangtalan, for example, resolution would have been easier because those villages held peace-pacts in common and also had many kinship ties. Second, the man had stolen things many times before, but this was the biggest theft yet. The last time he was caught stealing, the *pangat* had warned there would be no leniency for subsequent crimes. If he stole again, he would be killed.

Dangtalan, a neutral site roughly halfway between Dalupa and Guina-ang, agreed to host the *pangat* deliberations. This time the man's fate was determined in the plaza. I arrived after speeches were well under way and sat on a log like many of the interested villagers. Several men stood up in turn to talk, but the most impassioned was Bill's primary assistant. Roberto was a wealthy and respected member of the community, and his performance was impressive. As his speech lengthened he grew angry and punched the air to emphasize his points. I looked around for someone to translate and saw another of Bill's assistants quietly watching. When I went over he said that Roberto was recounting all the things this man had stolen and the many chances he had already received. Roberto recounted the last time they met regarding this fellow and emphasized the *pangat*'s earlier decision to render an ultimatum. He concluded by saying that there was no option now but to carry out the previous edict. The NPA should be informed of the case and requested to carry out the execution, which I learned later had been done on other occasions.

Roberto finally sat down, his face apoplectic. I was horrified. Until then I had been in complete agreement with the Kalinga form of justice, believing it was superior to the American system. But killing a person for stealing seemed too harsh. From what I had heard, this man was a confirmed kleptomaniac. Yet all his thefts were so easily discovered that it appeared he was unable to control his urges. Was that a reason to kill him? As an anthropologist and an outside observer, I knew that I should not intervene, though I was tempted to speak out and suggest a solution such as financial compensation for the loss of the carabao. Instead I walked away from the meeting and learned from others that the *pangat* had indeed followed Roberto's urgent appeal. At any rate the man was in hiding so the sentence could not be carried out immediately.

I returned to Guina-ang that night distraught that I had just witnessed a directive to execute someone for stealing. In addition, I was awed by the power of the *pangat*. Unlike the rape case, no one asked me how I felt about this decision, which I took as a message to keep quiet.

A week went by and I heard nothing more of the matter. Still, I continued to be tormented by my decision not to intervene. The only comfort was that my opinion probably didn't matter, although I knew I would have felt better if I had spoken. I waited anxiously each day to hear whether the sentence had been carried out. Finally, I could stand it no longer and asked one of my assistants what had happened to the man. They told me that Roberto and the other *pangat* did inform the NPA of the death sentence, but then Roberto gave the man some money so he could flee to the city. I was extremely relieved. What a marvelous solution for a repeat offender. If he was dumb enough to come back to the Pasil Valley he would probably be killed, but if he just stayed away his life could be spared. He might have continued to steal in the city and could now be rotting in an urban jail, but I was impressed again by the way the Kalinga resolved a conflict and restored harmony to their communities.

Fortunately or not, my inclination to participate in dispute resolution was fulfilled following an incident that involved one of the anthropology students and a young Kalinga man. As part of the project we occasionally had a number of Filipino undergraduate students stay with us for a short time. A university education in the Philippines was for the most part still limited to upper-class families. Our student visitors from Manila usually represented the highest strata of the Filipino social structure. Bill asked if several of the students could stay in Guina-ang for a short time, which seemed like a good idea, but within two days of their arrival there was already a crisis. The problem began when some of the young Guina-ang women became smitten with one of the students who initiated what he considered a harmless flirtation. The blood of the young Kalinga men rose. Because I was so involved in my own research and had seen none of this activity, what happened next caught me off guard. While I slept soundly in my bed, several Kalinga men poured gin on the flames of their jealousy, and one of them burst into the house of the sleeping students, put a gun to the head of Romeo and said coldly, "I'm going to kill you now." Luckily, several children scurried off to wake Joseph and Amboy, who arrived within seconds and managed to disarm the would-be assailant. I slept right through it because Joseph, Amboy, and the rest of the villagers were too embarrassed to tell me and the students were too scared to leave their house until daylight.

One of the female students came to my house at first light. I went over and found the fellow extremely shaken but seemingly unaware of why it had happened. I too was baffled, and as I huddled with my assistants who described the night's events I knew it would be an unusual day. I met with several *pangat* who initially apologized and insisted that the gun-toting Kalinga man be punished. As was typical, the man had left the village to let the two parties work out a compromise. In this case I had to serve as the negotiating *pangat* for the Filipino students, given that they were my guests in the village. I spent the day in diplomatic shuttle between houses. The Filipino student just wanted to go home. The Kalinga view seemed to be that the gunman should apologize and hold a feast to make amends for his actions. By late afternoon it looked like an agreement had been reached and the Kalinga man was forced to butcher a dog for a meal that would be attended by both parties. The student reluctantly agreed, made a brief appearance, ate some food, shook the hand of the Kalinga man, and then retreated to his house.

I thought it was over and everyone was satisfied until one of the *pangat* sat down next to me to say how much they liked me and how out of respect for me they would permit the students to stay in the village. This was my first hint that there was more to the story. Joseph was also there so I questioned him about the day previous to the incident, which had not been mentioned at all to me during our negotiations. He reluctantly told me about the flirting and how enraged all the young men were by the student's behavior, nice clothes, and superior air. Realizing that the issue was not yet resolved, I went back to the elderly man and asked him whether I should have the students leave Guina-ang. He shook his head yes. This, of course, was not really a problem. They had wanted to leave Guina-ang for the previous twelve hours, but now I would be asking them to leave and not return. Although it had taken me a while to understand the full story, I was pleased with the outcome. No single event during my stay demonstrated more clearly to the people of Guina-ang that I respected them and their ways.

Another way the Kalinga impressed me was in their treatment of individuals who simply did not fit the norm. A nearby village had an Episcopal church with a college-educated Kalinga minister. We had gotten acquainted at a couple of funerals and he invited me to mass and lunch. One sunny Sunday morning I thought it would be fun to take him up on the invitation, so Amboy and I hiked up to the village. We attended mass and then went to lunch at the minister's house, the largest in town.

We talked for a while on his porch before lunch. One of the people preparing and serving the meal caught my attention. These tasks were most often done by women, but it seemed that a man was bringing out the bowls of rice. Amboy shared my interest in the server and whispered in my ear, "That's really a woman." Like me, Amboy was also an outsider here and was keenly interested in this person, whom he knew only by reputation. I asked the minister about her later, and he said the woman dressed like a man and spent a lot of time doing men's work but that she was able to perform in a female's role when necessary, as in the case of meal preparation. She was neither derided nor ostracized but accepted as a contributing member of society.

The village of Guina-ang also had a man who I would guess would be labeled by our psychological community as clinically insane. In Guina-ang it was impossible to miss him. His hair was long and snarled into a tortuous mess, and he was usually quite filthy. That, plus his Charles Manson stare, gave him a somewhat startling appearance. He was middle-aged, living alone in a small house, which had either been owned by his deceased parents or given to him by someone in the community. The man did not have rice fields, do fieldwork, or help otherwise around the village. One could usually find him on his porch, although he did occasionally participate in our nightly basketball games. I did not pay much attention to him but one day during my research, which included an evening meal with a family, he entered the house and sat down. He was served without comment and ate quietly. He stayed for a while after dinner and then disappeared. My curiosity piqued, I asked Amboy and Joseph about his situation. They stated that they too thought the man was insane but that he would take his meals at a number of houses where his occasional appearance at dinner was accepted. This was less an intrusion in Kalinga society since it was acceptable for neighbors, friends, and especially children to join other households for dinner without invitation.

In our society this person would be institutionalized or living on the streets.

CHAPTER 9

When a Town Gets a Road the People Go Crazy

I HAD DINNER late one afternoon with the mayor of the entire Pasil Valley, who was also the principal of the high school. He was a wealthy man living in one of the best houses in the valley and a *pangat* as well. Both he and his wife had college degrees and were very helpful during our stay. Our paths crossed only during area-wide events such as funerals, but on these occasions he served as my guide, explaining details of certain rituals and inviting me to participate when appropriate. In some ways the mayor and his wife exemplified an ideal response to the clash of two worlds: they sought outside education and higher degrees while proudly maintaining Kalinga cultural traditions.

One of the keys to cultural survival is self-determination, which the Kalinga have so far preserved by violent opposition to all outside encroachment. But merely gaining more control of one's fate does not insure group survival.

In my discussion with the mayor I asked him about the future. He responded that he believed strongly that a road on the north side of the Pasil Valley, which included Guina-ang, would be beneficial to all. This would be no small undertaking since it required a bridge across the river gorge and cutting a road into the mountainside to reach Guina-ang. I had not been impressed with the villages that already had a road and wondered whether the benefits for Guina-ang would be more imaginary than real, citing towns such as Ableg and Lubuagon as examples. He replied, "When a town gets a road the people go crazy." One could no longer go to those villages and feel safe, he said, nor was it possible to drop in on a distant relative and expect to be fed, a Kalinga barometer of community friendliness. To me, and apparently to the mayor, it seemed that there was a direct relationship between the arrival of a road and the breakdown of traditional Kalinga customs and values, the rise of lawlessness, and the inability of the *pangat* and the peace pacts to control social deviance. The thugs and holduppers always seemed to come from towns blessed by a road. Then why? I asked. "We'll be smarter than that," he said.

It often happens that even when a group has the power to determine its own course, it encounters unexpected and overwhelming forces for change and assimilation. Yet if any group can negotiate such forces, it will be the Kalinga, who have successfully maintained their cultural identity over hundreds of years of Western contact.

Since the fifteenth century, European expansion and colonization have created conditions for collision with indigenous peoples everywhere, almost always to the detriment of the latter. Thousands of ethnic groups have completely vanished through a combination of introduced diseases, which killed up to 50 percent of indigenous people in some parts of the world; acculturation leading to the loss of traditional language and culture; or in the most extreme cases genocide. Certain native groups in California, for example, were hunted and killed like varmints as settlers moved in and claimed the land for themselves. This is a pattern repeated in many parts of the world. In Tasmania sheep herders coveted land that had been occupied by a people for thousands of years; the army hunted them down, and the survivors were confined to missions where they all eventually died. A complete ethnic group was thus exterminated in a matter of decades. Events like these are part of an ugly chapter in world history, and they should not be forgotten. Racism and bigotry are still prevalent in our society. Fear and hatred of difference are but one small step from the inhumane treatment and, in fact, tolerance of genocide.

The discipline of anthropology was established, in part, to record and preserve non-Western cultures before they were greatly changed through European contact, or eliminated altogether. Anthropologists swarmed over the globe in the early part of the twentieth century recording traditional languages, religions, subsistence techniques, and all other lifestyle elements. Yet no human society is static, and it may be a Western presumption that cultures can or should be preserved like specimens. What I am advocating is simply the right of any people to choose its own path. The early anthropologists did not foresee that by the beginning of the twenty-first century non-European cultural traditions would have endured, though often changed dramatically. Now anthropology has assumed a more active role in trying to ensure the rights of remaining indigenous people in the face of development and continuing exploitation. Most active has been Cultural Survival, founded in 1972 by David Maybury-Lewis. Cultural Survival investigates human-rights abuses and assists peoples in taking charge of their own future. Unfortunately, there are massive economic and cultural forces working against such efforts and failures outnumber successes.

The Kalinga are often cited as an example of a people that has successfully maintained identity and homeland while many other indigenous groups in the Philippines have disappeared under the same onslaught. Why have the Kalinga survived? Two reasons are obvious. First, the Kalinga have a well-deserved reputation for aggression, and any overt external threat—be it a neighboring tribe or the Philippine military—is met with force. Their guerrilla tactics were highly successful in preventing showcase hydroelectric projects, especially after they traded in their head axes for automatic weapons. Going toe-to-toe with a modern army is risky business; many groups around the world that reacted in similar fashion have been annihilated. In this case, the Kalinga were successful for the same reason that the Viet Cong ultimately prevailed against the American military machine during the Vietnam war. Modern armies are simply ineffective in jungle terrain against committed resistance.

Second, the Kalinga are isolated. The rugged mountains have made it difficult to penetrate the region even today. This has bought the Kalinga time. The first indigenous groups in the Philippines to lose their land were those living in easily reached areas with exploitable natural resources. The Kalinga region does contain gold and a mine operated successfully for some time, but the demanding logistical considerations are still a huge negative factor in further development. Because the Kalinga have demonstrated that they will quickly resort to violence if their land is threatened, and because no corporation so far has been willing to incur the costs of establishing an infrastructure, the Kalinga have been left to incorporate or reject outside influences at their own pace.

So far the Kalinga have managed to negotiate the tide of outside cultural forces. Recognizing the value of education, many families since the 1970s have sent at least one family member to college. Today, all the teachers in the Pasil Valley are Kalinga. There are also Kalinga lawyers, dentists, government officials, and even an anthropologist. No single choice has had a greater effect on their survival. Armed resistance is probably not the answer any longer, but what may allow them to control their future are dozens of college-educated Kalinga, people like the Pasil Valley mayor, who can help mediate outside influences. One of these days Guina-ang will get a road, but the people will not go crazy.

Bibliography

CHAPTER 1

Asian Forum on Human Rights
1980   *The Uprooting of a People in Kalinga-Apayao: Chico River Hydroelectric Project.* AFHR, Hong Kong.

Binford, Lewis R.
1978   *Nunamiut Ethnoarchaeology.* Academic Press, New York.

Fiagoy, Geraldine
1987   *Death Stalks the Isneg.* Cordillera Papers (Vol. 1, Nos. 3 and 4). Cordillera Consultation and Research, Baguio City.

Kidder, Alfred V.
1924   *An Introduction to the Study of Southwestern Archaeology with a Preliminary Account of the Excavations at Pecos.* Yale University Press, New Haven.

Kramer, Carol
1982   *Village Ethnoarchaeology: Rural Iran in Archaeological Perspective.* Academic Press, New York.

Longacre, William A.
1970   Archaeology as Anthropology: A Case Study. *Anthropological Papers of the University of Arizona 17.* University of Arizona Press, Tucson.

1974   Kalinga Pottery-making: The Evolution of a Research Design. In *Frontiers of Anthropology*, edited by Murray J. Leaf, pp. 51–67. D. Van Nostrand, New York.

1981   Kalinga Pottery: An Ethnoarchaeological Study. In *Patterns of the Past: Studies in Honour of David Clarke*, edited by I. Hodder, G. Isaac, and N. Hammond, pp. 49–66. Cambridge University Press, London.

1991   *Ceramic Ethnoarchaeology.* University of Arizona Press, Tucson.

Longacre, William A., and James M. Skibo (editors)
1995   *Kalinga Ethnoarchaeology: Expanding Archaeological Method and Theory.* Smithsonian Institution Press, Washington, D.C.

Skibo, James M.
1992   *Pottery Function: A Use-alteration Approach.* Plenum Publishing, New York.

Woodbury, Richard B.
1973   *Alfred Kidder.* Columbia University Press, New York.

Chapter 2

Bain, David Haward
1984   *Sitting in Darkness: Americans in the Philippines.* Houghton Mifflin, Boston.

Karnow, Stanley
1989   *In Our Image: America's Empire in the Philippines.* Random House, New York.

Levesque, Rodrigue
1980   *The Philippines: Pigafetta's Story of Their Discovery by Magellan.* Levesque Publications, Quebec.

Perez, Telesforo Carrasco
1986   *A Spaniard in Aguinaldo's Army.* Solar Publishing, Manila (translated by Nick Joaquin).

Semenov, Sergei A.
1964   *Prehistoric Technology* (translated by M. W. Thompson). Cory, Adams and Mackay, London.

Sternber, David Joel
1994   *The Philippines: A Singular and Plural Place.* Westview Press, Boulder.

Wolff, Leon
1970   *Little Brown Brother.* Longmans, New York.

Zwick, Jim
1992   *Mark Twain's Weapon of Satire: Anti-Imperialist Writings on the Philippine-American War.* Syracuse University Press, Syracuse.

Chapter 3

Agoncillo, Teodoro A.
1975   *A Short History of the Philippines.* New American Library, New York.

Barton, R. F.
1930   *The Half-Way Sun: Life Among the Headhunters of the Philippines.* Brewer and Warren, New York.

1949   *The Kalingas, Their Institutions and Custom Law.* University of Chicago Press, Chicago.

Bellwood, Peter
1979   *Man's Conquest of the Pacific.* Oxford University Press, New York.

1985   *Prehistory of the Indo-Malaysian Archipelago.* Academic Press, New York.

1987   *The Polynesians: Prehistory of an Island People.* Thames and Hudson, London.

Bondoc, Nester H.
1979   A Re-investigation of the Espinosa Archaeological Sites: Cagayan and Kalinga-Apayao. *Anthropological Papers No. 6,* National Museum, Manila.

Dozier, Edward P.
1966   *Mountain Arbiters: The Changing Life of a Philippine Hill People.* University of Arizona Press, Tucson.

Fagan, Brian
1990   *The Journey from Eden.* Thames and Hudson, London

Fox, Robert B.
1967   *Pre-history of the Philippines.* National Museum, Manila.

1970   *The Tabon Caves.* Monograph No. 1, National Museum, Manila.

Malinowski, Bronislaw
1967   *A Diary in the Strict Sense of the Term.* Harcourt, Brace and World, New York.

Murdock, George P.
1945   The Common Denominator of Cultures. In *The Science of Man in the World of Crisis.* Columbia University Press, New York.

Scott, William Henry
1984   *Prehispanic Source Materials for the Study of Philippine History.* New Day Publishers, Quezon City.

1994   *Barangay: Sixteenth-century Philippine Culture and Society.* Ateneo de Manila Press, Quezon City.

Sugguiyao, Miguel
1990   *The Kalinga Hilltribe of the Philippines.* Office of Northern Cultural Communities, Manila.

Worcester, Dean C.
1912   Headhunters of Northern Luzon. *National Geographic* 23:833–930.

1913   The Non-Christian Tribes of the Philippines. *National Geographic* 24:1157–1256.

Worcester, Dean C., and R. Hayden
1930   *The Philippines Past and Present.* Macmillan, New York.

Chapter 4

De Raedt, Jules
1989   *Kalinga Sacrifices.* Cordillera Monograph 4, University of the Philippines, College Baguio, Baguio City.

Dozier, Edward P.
1966   *Mountain Arbiters.* University of Arizona Press, Tucson.

Hoy, Suellen
1995   *Chasing Dirt: The American Pursuit of Cleanliness.* Oxford Univesity Press, Oxford.

Lawless, Robert
1983   On First Being an Anthropologist. In *Fieldwork: The Human Experience*, edited by R. Lawless, V. H. Sutlive, Jr., and M. D. Zamora, pp. 19–34. Gordon and Breach, New York.

Magannon, Esteban T.
1972   *Religion in a Kalinga Village: Its Implications for Planned Change.* Community Development Research Council, University of the Philippines, Quezon City.

Miner, Horace
1956   Body Ritual Among the Nacirema. *American Anthropologist* 58.

Wright, Lawrence
1960   *Clean and Decent: The Fascinating History of the Bathroom and Water Closet.* Routledge and Kegan Paul, London.

Chapter 5

Leakey, Richard, and Roger Lewin
1996   *The Sixth Extinction: Patterns of Life and the Future of Humankind.* Anchor Books, New York.

Martin, Paul S.
1975   Philosophy of Education at Vernon Field Station. In *Fieldiana Anthropology* Vol. 65, "Chapters in the Prehistory of Eastern Arizona," IV, pp.3–11. Field Musum of Natural History, Chicago.

McGregor, John C.
1965   *Southwestern Archaeology*. University of Illinois Press, Urbana.

Schiffer, Michael Brian
1996   *Behavioral Archaeology: First Principles.* University of Utah Press, Salt Lake City.

Skibo, James M., and Gary Feinman (editors)
1999   *Pottery and People: A Dynamic Interaction.* University of Utah Press, Salt Lake City.

Skibo, James M., William H. Walker, and Axel E. Nielsen (editors)
1995   *Expanding Archaeology.* University of Utah Press, Salt Lake City.

Streuver, Stuart, and Felicia Antonelli Holton
1979   *Koster: Americans in Search of their Prehistoric Past.* Anchor Press, New York.

Thomas, Cyrus
1985   (orig. 1894) *Report on the Mound Explorations of the Bureau of Ethnology.* Smithsonian Institution Press, Washington, D.C.

Willey, Gordon R., and Jeremy A. Sabloff
1993   *A History of American Archaeology* (3rd edition). W. H. Freeman, San Francisco.

Chapter 6

Brown, Donald E.
1990   The Penis Pin. In *Female and Male in Borneo: Contributions and Challenges to Gender Studies,* edited by V. Sutlive, pp. 435–454. The Borneo Research Council.

Callender, Charles, and Lee M. Kochems
1987   The North American Berdache. *Current Anthropology* 24:443–456.

Ford, C. S., and F. A. Beach
1951   *Patterns of Sexual Behavior.* Harper Torchbooks, New York.

Herdt, Gilbert H.
1984   *Ritualized Homosexuality in Melanesia.* University of California Press, Berkeley.

Chapter 7

Diamond, Jared
1997   *Guns, Germs, and Steel: The Fates of Human Societies.* W. W. Norton, New York.

Chapter 8

Scott, William Henry
1987   *Chips.* New Day Publishers, Quezon City.

Acknowledgments

A NUMBER OF PEOPLE and institutions deserve acknowl-
edgment for their contributions to this volume. The Kalinga
Ethnoarchaeological Project was supported by a number of grants
from the National Science Foundation: SOC 75-19006, BNS 87-
10275, BNS 89-01797, and BNS 89-15359. Special thanks go to
both the Anthropology and Archaeology divisions of the National
Museum of the Philippines in Manila, the departments of anthropology at the University of Arizona, Illinois State University, and
the University of the Philippines, the Arizona State Museum, and
especially the Laboratory of Traditional Technology.

The members of the Kalinga Ethnoarchaeological Project share
in this story. They include Masashi Kobayashi, Miriam Stark, Ramon
Silvestre, Brian Trostel, Chris Turner, and José Lorde Villamor. We
are also very grateful to all of our Kalinga assistants and friends,
some of whom include Roberta and Christina Tima, Amboy
Lingbawan, Joseph Abacan, Nancy Lugao, Edita Lugao, Judith
Sagayo, Iya Lingbawan, Thomasa Dawagon, and John and Delia
Sawil. These Pasil Valley residents and others made our stay safe
and pleasant.

Many people read all or part of this manuscript or in some way
contributed to making it a better book. They are Mary Fran, Rob-
ert and Marc Bjork, Dave Brown, Marla Buckmaster, Robert Dirks,
Karen, Allison, and Kimberly Fell, James Johnson, Bill Longacre,
Bob Mangialardi, Fr. Larry Morlan, Martin Nickels, Charles Orser,
Mike Schiffer, Becky Skibo, Matt and Rose Mae Skibo, James
Stanlaw, Mary Van Buren, and Bill Walker.

Four people need to be singled out for their contributions. Bill Longacre, Director of the Kalinga Ethnoarchaeological Project, invited me to participate in the study, taught me how to be an ethnoarchaeologist, read several drafts of this manucript, and has served as wonderful mentor and friend. He is probably more qualified to write this book than I. Mike Schiffer has also been an unfailing mentor and friend. His ceaseless encouragement convinced me to see this project through to completion. His evil blue pen also made this book better. Jeff Grathwohl, Director of the University of Utah Press, not only encouraged me to write this book but was personally involved at every stage and even served as the editor, an unusual task for a Director. A good editor, he told me, makes a book five percent better. His thoughtful suggestions, along with the help of Rodger Reynolds and the rest of the Utah staff, did at least that.

Finally, my wife, Becky, deserves the highest thanks. She lived through the fieldwork experience and served as a silent coauthor, and her constant encouragement made this book come to life. When I was questioning whether to write a book like this and whether anyone would publish or read it, she told me not to worry and just write it for our kids. Because those words inspired me throughout its creation, I dedicate this book to our wonderful children, Matt and Sadie.

About the Author

JAMES SKIBO is associate professor of anthropology at Illinois State University, Normal, Illinois, and co-director, with William Walker, of La Frontera Archaeological Program. He is the author of *Pottery Function*, and is the editor of *Pottery and People: A Dynamic Interaction* (Utah 1999) and *Expanding Archaeology* (Utah 1995).